(Courtesy University of Maine)

The University of Maine's Flagship Campus
Orono, Maine

SUPER U

SUPER U:

THE HISTORY AND POLITICS

of the

UNIVERSITY OF MAINE SYSTEM

by
James Delmas Libby, Ph.D.

PICTON PRESS
ROCKPORT, MAINE

All rights reserved
Copyright © 2000 Picton Press
International Standard Book Number 0-89725-419-8
Library of Congress Catalog Card Number 00-109514

No part of this publication may be reproduced, stored in a retrieval system, or transmitted in any form or by any means whatsoever, including electronic, mechanical, magnetic recording, the Internet, or photocopying, without the prior written approval of the Copyright holder, excepting brief quotations for inclusion in book reviews.

First Printing December 2000

This book is available from:
James D. Libby, Ph.D.
88 Union Falls Road
Buxton, ME 04093

For Signed Copies:
(207) 929-5987

This book is also available from:
Picton Press
PO Box 250
Rockport, ME 04856-0250

Visa/MasterCard orders: 1-207-236-6565
FAX orders: 1-207-236-6713
www.pictonpress.com

Manufactured in the United States of America
Printed on 60# acid-free paper

TABLE OF CONTENTS

List of Figures ix

List of Tables ix

Preface xi

Acknowledgments xiii

Chapter One: Introduction 1
   Purpose of the Study 1
   Overview of Single-State Analysis 2

Chapter Two: Literature Review 5
   Part One: Governance Theory in Higher Education 5
      State Structures 5
      Autonomy and Accountability 9
   Part Two: The Maine System 15
      Historical Development 15
      Current Structure 23

Chapter Three: Research Problem and Method 27
   Conceptual Framework 27
   Subject Matter and Scope 28
   Research Design 29
   Developing the Research Questions 31
   Primary Research Questions and Propositions 37
   The Political Interventions Model 38
   Threats to Validity 43

Chapter Four: Growth and Development of the University of
   Maine System 45
   Introduction to the Political History 45
   The First Phase: The Early Years (1968-1974) 47
      The Administration of Governor **Kenneth M. Curtis**
      (1967-1974) 47

The Term of Chancellor **Don McNeil** (1969-1974) 52
The Second Phase: 1975-1986 56
   The Term of Acting Chancellor **Stanley L. Freeman**
     (12/1974-8/1975) 56
   The Administration of Governor **James B. Longley**
     (1975-1978) 60
   The Term of Chancellor **Patrick E. McCarthy** (1975-1986) . 66
   The Administration of Governor **Joseph E. Brennan**
     (1979-1986) 78
   The Term of Chancellor **Jack E. Freeman**
     (7/1/1986-7/16/1986) 82
The Third Phase: 1987- 2000 85
   The Term of Chancellor **Robert L. Woodbury** (1986-1993) . 86
   The Administration of Governor **John R. McKernan, Jr.**
     (1987-1994) 93
   The Term of Chancellor **J. Michael Orenduff** (1993-1996) . 102
   The Administration of Governor **Angus S. King, Jr.**
     (1995-Present) 109
   The Term of Chancellor **Terrence MacTaggart**
     (1996-Present) 116

Chapter Five: Analysis 135
   Principles of Analysis 135
   The Political Interventions Model 136
     Part One: Defining Attempted Political Intervention 138
     Part Two: Identification of Issues 140
     Part Three: Identification of Responsible Political Intervener 141
     Part Four: Results 142
     Part Five: Findings 143
   Summary of Political Interventions Model 146
   Responding to the Research Questions 147
   Accountability and Founding Expectations 148

Chapter Six: Conclusion 153
   Public Accountability and the University of Maine System 153
   Governor's Role in Maine Higher Education 155
   System Relationship to State Government 156
   Implications 157

References 161

Appendix A: The Longley Veto 173

Appendix B: The Freeman Resignation 177

Appendix C: Portraits of Governors and Chancellors Presiding Over
 the University of Maine System 179

Biography of the Author 192

Every Name Index 193

LIST OF FIGURES

Figure 2.1: The Consolidated Governing Board Structure of the Maine System 24

Figure 3.1: Basic Types of Designs for Case Studies 30

Figure 4.1: Communication Flows: Commission on Higher Education Governance 121

Figure 5.1: Model of Political Intervention Analysis 136

LIST OF TABLES

Table 3.1: Kinds of Data Collected and Inferences Drawn 40

Table 3.2: Major Reports, University of Maine System 41, 42

Table 4.1: Chancellors Installed for the University of Maine System 46

Table 5.1: Issues of Political Significance to the University System 140

Table 5.2: Identification of Political Interveners 141

Table 5.3: Action Resulting from the Forceful Political Interventions 142, 143

PREFACE

It is my hope that this book will serve many future generations as an historical accounting of the progress of the University of Maine System from its birth in 1968 to the year A.D. 2000. My original purpose for writing it was to help fulfill the requirements for a Ph.D. from the University of Maine. I have had the good fortune of gaining some positive reviews on the work, however imperfect, and as a result I offer it to you in this book version.

I have come to believe as a result of this work that the State of Maine has something to be proud of in the University of Maine System. However high the tuition, however tense the labor, however limited the offerings, for the most part, the University of Maine System has served its people. The extent to which our government is responsible for the level of its effectiveness is one topic that will be explored in this book.

The writing is technical at times. For those of you that wish to simply enjoy a recounting and analysis of the University of Maine System, you may want to skim the first few sections and go on to the history of the System, located part way through Chapter 2. You will find an account of governors, chancellors, a few board members and legislators, all of which have labored over the direction of the multi-campus system.

This single-state case study establishes a procedure to evaluate the effectiveness of actions taken by a unified structure of public higher education governance in response to forceful political interventions by government entities. One state's attempt to assure sustainable, efficient, and effective operations within a statutorily created governing board structure was critically explored.

The study employed content analysis to verify, examine, and explain a variety of historical events using several sources of evidence. The first phase of this research explored the growth and development of the State of Maine's system of public higher education from its birth, effectively documenting the history and politics of the University of Maine System since its establishment in 1968. Each of Maine's governors and chancellors that have presided over the system were profiled. Important board actions of system trustees were investigated, with special emphasis on their response to political pressures for policy redirection. Maine state government's oversight responsibility was contrasted with the ability of its university system to plot a course of its own within a unified, single-board format of governance, while at the same time responding to public demands expressed through Maine's chief executives, its legislatures, and its citizens.

As a result of this analysis, a relationship was found to exist between various levels of political interventions in Maine and associated policy resolutions. The study concluded that the unified system of higher education governance in Maine is pliable and resilient, and that its flexibility to political demands successfully relieved external pressures to overhaul the system. Most surprising of all, however, was the discovery that despite the governance successes associated with the System's resilient structure, many goals established for the System by its founders have yet to be achieved.

ACKNOWLEDGEMENTS

I would like to offer my deepest thanks to my family for the support that they have given to me during the past several years while I have completed this work. I'm sure that each of them believed at this point that I was destined to be a perennial student. Fortunately, this chapter of my life has concluded prior to age forty.

I would also like to thank my Committee members for the guidance that they offered and for their leadership in the fields of public policy and higher education. To Deans Cobb and Weschler, Professors Brown and McIntire, your comments and suggestions displayed startling brilliance. Most of all I would like to thank my Committee Chair, Professor Jean Lavigne: you have had a profound effect on me.

While I have done my utmost to incorporate the scientific instruments of the trade, this work may somewhere reflect the commitments or philosophy inherent in my background. I have relied on the expert opinion of my Committee to mitigate this variable, but those who agree or disagree with the content and conclusions of this research will surely note the author's elected position and political party affiliation. I have found my position as an officeholder helpful in gaining a richer understanding of the subject.

CHAPTER ONE: INTRODUCTION

> *In this subject as in others, the best method of investigation is to study things in the process of development from the beginning.*
>
> Aristotle
> In: *Presidents, Professors, and Trustees*, Cowley, 1980, p. 9

Purpose of the Study

This book offers a single-state case study of a unified structure of public higher education, concentrating specifically on how the structure has responded to political interventions. The state system chosen for this study was the University of Maine System.

Just twenty or thirty years ago, there were those who frowned at a single-state analysis of higher education governance. However, as the century drew to a close, researchers and analysts generated more single-state cases than ever before, and for good reason; they are being read by practitioners, researchers, critics, and other interested parties.

The value of the single-state analysis of public higher education's structural effectiveness is realized on several fronts. An historical approach to the case-study method tracks important changes over time and provides policymakers with a basis upon which to make future decisions. For example, newly appointed trustees find case studies to be an essential tool for review of their system. In states where major restructuring has taken place in higher education governance, a case study can be a reference point for the new governing bodies. In states with term-limited legislatures, the historically based case study can provide a new member of a legislature's education committee, for example, with an important framework for critical votes. Candidates for chief executive positions turn to these studies for important insights into a system's track record and future needs. Finally, the single-state analysis provides important data for national leaders whose job it is to provide comparative analysis on at least two levels: between individual states and between states with similar governance structures.

The most notable national research of this kind is the recent and well-known comprehensive case study summary approach employed by the California Higher Education Policy Center. The Center constructed an analysis entitled, "The State Structures for the Governance of Higher Education Series," which has synthesized case studies; historical analyses; interviews; government and university information; and newspaper, periodical, and other important political, economic, and social data (Bowen, Bracco, Callan, Finney, Richarson, Jr., & Trombley, 1997). The Center's final product has documented single-state snapshots and provided comprehensive comparative analysis.

States including California, Florida, Georgia, Illinois, Michigan, New York, and Texas have all been involved in the California Policy Center's case-study process, and the end product has not only been well received, but also is now quickly becoming a starting point from which policymakers have buttressed analyses of their own states.

Overview of Single-State Analysis

Various sources of widely scattered information have been used to assist national and state researchers in the examination of the thirty-two-year-old unified governance mechanism operating Maine's public university system. In the State of Maine, no previous comprehensive historical documentation exists of the events, decisions, players, successes, failures, opportunities, and missed opportunities that have taken place during the life of its public university system. Without a baseline document, the internal and external pressures to improve or to change this system may be haphazardly interpreted by those without the benefit of institutional memory. The reader of this research will have the opportunity to be informed about the past, present, and possibly even the future political environment of public higher education in the state of Maine, and that kind of informed position tends to promote policy-making efficacy.

The end product of this research has differed from that of the California Higher Education Policy Center initiative in many important ways. First, this research focuses specifically on the history, disposition, and structural effectiveness of the University of Maine System. Although this research serves as an effective history of the University of Maine

1: Introduction

System's governance and politics, history is only the first component of this study. Second, as a technical research paper, this study serves as "a critical case in testing a well-formulated theory" by examining the effect of external political interventions upon the University of Maine System (Yin, 1994, p. 38). Few studies have tracked a system's resiliency to these interventions despite numerous references in academic literature to rising levels of external influence. In other words, this research project explored "systemic pliancy," or how flexible and responsive a state's system of higher education governance is in the face of public pressure. By way of comparison, the research conducted by the California Higher Education Policy Center was much broader in its focus and was designed to provide a present-day snapshot of the condition of higher education for each state at that moment in time, with historical foundations also provided. The Center's individual research of each state was later used for comparative analysis among the states that participated (for more information, see Bowen, et al., 1997).

This research then documents the deliberative movements of the University of Maine System from its birth in 1968 to the end of the century. In addition to the analysis of this System, it is specifically designed to furnish policymakers with the foundation necessary to develop a perspective specific to the fiscal, legal, historical, and intellectual integrity of other systems. National researchers will be able to use this model to structure an analysis of "systemic pliancy." In addition, all interested parties may access this document as a supplement to their own activities, and they should be able to easily synthesize it with other important policy-specific information not referenced in this document. By examining the successes and the growing pains of a single-state public university system over its entire history, this research provides a richer understanding of the political ramifications of a unified state governance structure (please consult Chapter Two for a detailed explanation of statewide governance structures).

CHAPTER TWO: LITERATURE REVIEW

> *...the politician determines the boundaries in which higher education will function, yet seldom do they focus on any of the available research on higher education...*
>
> Caprice Brown, *Governance of Higher Education in Louisiana: The Process and Impact of Politics*, 1993, p. 191

Part One: Governance Theory in Higher Education

State Structures

There are a myriad of governance approaches in higher education throughout the fifty states, Puerto Rico, and the District of Columbia. Each has developed over time, based on individual state needs, political pressures, and historical relationships. In general, though, differences between state structures are usually classified into three basic categories: consolidated governing boards, coordinating boards, and planning agencies.

States with planning agencies vary, but usually maintain a functional oversight group leading voluntary planning efforts or licensing requirements. Very few states employ this method, but in New England, Maine's closest neighbors of Vermont and New Hampshire appear to effectively govern their systems in this manner. In contrast with Maine, Vermont's voluntary planning agency does not have the statutory authority of a board of trustees. For example, program or budget approval is handled by the centralized trustee system in Maine, but not in Vermont (McGuinness, 1994). New Hampshire maintains a hybrid system, with some aspects of both planning agency and statewide governance (McGuinness, 1994).

Maine is most often referred to as a consolidated governing board state. Some researchers refer to this structure as a unified or central governance system; therefore, the terms will be used interchangeably.

According to Aims McGuinness of the National Center for Higher Education Management Systems, a consolidated governing board:
- usually heads a single corporate entity that encompasses all institutions within the system
- carries out coordinating responsibilities in addition to its responsibilities for governing institutions under its jurisdiction
- has authority both to develop and implement policy
- advocates for the needs of the institutions to the legislature and governor
- appoints, sets compensation for, and evaluates system and institutional chief executives
- sets faculty personnel policies and usually approves tenure
- has authority to allocate and reallocate resources between and among the institutions within its jurisdiction
- establishes policies for and, in some cases, sets tuition and fees (McGuinness, 1994, p. 6)

This description compares closely with Maine statutes, although Maine trustees have little coordinating oversight outside their jurisdiction. More than twenty other states join Maine in employing governing boards, including some states demographically comparable to Maine. Examples of these states include South Dakota, Rhode Island, Montana, and Idaho.

Another twenty states operate under the formal structure of a coordinating board. Coordinating-board states are characterized by a decentralized approach, in which each campus is allowed to have its own regulatory board with either full program approval authority, such as in Connecticut, Maryland, South Carolina, and Arkansas, or a strong program advisory responsibility, such as in Nebraska, Colorado, and Washington (McGuinness, 1994, p. 6). Coordinating board systems can be complex and are also sometimes referred to as federal systems. They may have some campuses with their own boards, while others are consolidated under a governing board that is subject to the coordinating board.

In recent years there were attempts by members of the general public and the Maine Legislature to move toward a more decentralized

2: Literature Review

approach such as that represented by a coordinating-board structure. So far, the university community, legislators, and others have resisted. This movement was probably captured best in Carlisle's (1996) report, "The University of Maine System: A Time for Change":

> While systems with consolidated governing boards may have served a valuable purpose in the past, current conditions suggest that their utility has expired. Research indicates that states that have returned governing powers to the individual institutions have enjoyed greater success in terms of quality of education and economic savings, while states that have maintained or strengthened their systems of central governance have continued a downward trend in quality. Not only is decentralization the sensible solution theoretically and statistically, but it also is aligned with the tradition of American higher education. (Carlisle, Wells, & Fitzgerald, 1996, p. 3)

As a result of the heavy pressure reflected in reports such as this one, Maine recently instituted a Board of Visitors at each campus. The board of visitor's concept in Maine does not yet allow these campus groups to exert a great deal of control over their institution. It appears that the concept of a weak visiting board might assist in providing a campus the wherewithal to promote and improve fund-raising efforts. This small change in the Maine System stands in contrast to larger restructuring efforts, such as the New Jersey experience documented later.

One example of a board of visitors' approach that encourages campus autonomy through delegated decision-making powers was described in "The University of Maine System: A Time for Change." This privately funded research project was quite critical of the University of Maine System's operations and structure:

> In Virginia, each institution has its own Board of Visitors, with control over the institution. Each institution allocates the money appropriated to it by the State as it sees fit. The institutions turn their tuition revenues over to the State and the State earns interest and later returns it to the University as a supplementary appropriation. The institutions retain control of

their endowment and gifts. Similar to Michigan, Virginia has one of the best institutions in the country. (Carlisle et al., 1996, pp. 13-14)

The report goes on to back up these statements with statistical reasoning, defining a board of visitors' policy like the one used in Virginia as far more autonomous at the campus level than the policy that has recently been implemented in Maine. Would the Virginia system be the right system for Maine at this point in time? More research yielding expert analysis could assist Maine in understanding the ramifications of this question. The object of this work is to provide a foundation to assist policy writers who are beginning to address this type of question.

Interstate comparisons of the advantages of using coordinating boards over governing boards can get muddled, because each state does have intricate differences. In general, however, a comparison of coordinating boards and governing boards can be made. According to McGuinness, a coordinating board differs from a governing board in that it:

- does not govern institutions (e.g., appoint institutional chief executives or set faculty personnel policies)
- usually does not have corporate status independent of state government
- focuses more on state and system needs and priorities than on advocating the interests of the higher education community; as Berdahl describes the function, these boards serve as 'suitably sensitive mechanisms' providing for a continuing transmission of the state's interests to higher education and higher education's needs to the state (McGuinness, 1995, p. 7).

Coordinating boards vary as to whether budget recommendations are made to the governor or legislature on a system-wide or on an institutional basis. They also vary in their ability to mandate the review of existing programs (McGuinness, 1995, p. 7). The redeeming quality to advocates is the decentralized nature of the design, but opponents counter that too much competition for state funding between campuses results.

Autonomy and Accountability

Although claims are occasionally made that some state systems are superior to others, little documented evidence exists to support this notion because so little comparative research has been done on the subject. While there is plenty of documentation on what other states are doing, the available literature on the subject of the effectiveness of various governance structures around the nation tends to be simplistic. A few attempts tend to highlight demographic, geographic and other differences between states in assigning a reason for the evolution of their structures and in the examination of why one structure may appear to work well over another. Each state's needs govern the development of the agency structure, it is assumed; therefore, some researchers appear to believe that structural development is less important to examine than autonomy and accountability. This book does not make such assumptions.

What happens when the legislation and delegated powers assigned to a state governance structure prevent the healthy growth and evolution of its university? Do such environments indeed even exist? The research is mostly silent on this question, other than a few recent dissertations that will be discussed later. Can there be a way to demonstrate that this condition does or does not exist in a given state? Currently, this is an unknown area in which new research is desperately needed. Thus, this case study is offered with the hope that similar research conducted by others will follow.

The national research has also been spotty on the basic question of comparing structural interrelationships with state government. Newman's (1987) *Choosing Quality* is referenced often in this document, and is a classic study that is widely read by college administrators. Work in this area also improved in 1988 with the publication of a repetitively referenced document authored by Edward R. Hines (1988) and authorized by the Association for the Study of Higher Education entitled, "Higher Education and State Governments: Renewed Partnership, Cooperation, or Competition?" Since 1988, other individual states have been examined via studies and dissertations, culminating in 1997 when a major multi-state comparative paper was presented entitled, "State Structures for the Governance of Higher Education: A Comparative Study," by the California Higher Education Policy Center (Bowen, et al., 1997). These two bookend publications and several others that were researched between 1988 and 2000 are examined in this section.

Research in recent years appears to have escalated due to a perceived movement by state governments to play a larger role in policy-making for higher education. Although this movement is unproven, followers of this theory point to the major changes made to governance structures in states such as New Jersey, Minnesota, and North Dakota, to name a few. It is possible that political consternation about the independent nature of university decisions (or lack thereof), budget problems, and other issues may have caused a deeper examination of problems in higher education in some states. Each state system evolves based on the ebb and flow of a variety of political issues. As a result, the research evolves with it.

A period of insignificant responsiveness to the problems identified in *A Nation at Risk* (National Commission on Excellence in Education, 1983) and other publications followed by a fairly severe economic recession in the early 1990s may have forced the hand of politicians and state boards, causing them to attempt to intervene into the sometimes-encapsulated world of higher education and its administration. Based on the volume of research available on these issues, the case-study method combined with content analysis and an historical/anthropological approach gained strength as a preferred methodological means used to examine questions of this nature by the end of the century. The evidence used to back this statement follows.

Since 1988, the research on state structures and their relationship to efficiency, effectiveness, and accountability in the provision of higher education services has improved. Within an examination of public-policy matters in higher education, the level of acceptance of content research played a key role in learning more about the how and why of the human dimension of leadership operating within differing structural environments. With a new acceptance in higher education circles of this type of research came an increase in its activity. The university's interface with political environments has led some researchers interested in this area to prioritize qualitative approaches or to synthesize quantitative data with qualitative studies that provide new analytical depth to the research. The necessity of this type of work appears paramount.

Research by Hines included a diverse advisory board and a long list of consulting editors that, interestingly, included a member from the

2: Literature Review

State of Maine (Hines, 1988). Hines' research provided an in-depth analysis of state leadership in higher education, new developments in state financial support for higher education, state policy issues, and the changing relationship between state governments and higher education. It is widely recognized that his analysis of the relationship between higher education and state government is where his most significant contribution to the literature has been made to date. His emphasis on the development of a better partnership between the states and their higher education establishments is evidenced by a rededication to higher education lobbying efforts in some states. Consider the following passage defining the operational spectrum in the Hines analysis:

> A partnership is not possible under conditions of full accountability or complete autonomy, or when one side defines the relationship unilaterally. Full accountability occurs when higher education functions as a public agency, subject to the controls and regulations pertaining to any other public agency. Complete campus autonomy is achieved when government is uninvolved in campus affairs, other than providing some minimal level of financial support. Theoretically, either policy option is possible, but in operational terms neither option can be considered seriously. (Hines, 1988, p. 103)

The reality for Hines is that neither the state nor higher education officials should be working in a vacuum; rather, each entity is an intra-organizational schema maintaining a semi-hierarchical relationship to the other, characterized by each entity having partial authority over, and partial independence from, the other (Hines, 1988, p. 103). For example, the difference in the relationships between states and higher education institutions over an array of policy matters can range from a laissez-faire approach to strong and direct intervention and supervision, but the "modal pattern in higher education has been for the state-aided or encouragement approach" (Hines, p. 105).

Both Hines and Newman have made the case for shared decision-making as well. This strand in the literature had a strong presence in the research in Maine, even as recently as the findings of an internal 1997 University of Maine System study entitled, "The Strategic Environmental Assessment." More on this report will be presented later in this research.

Newman cultivated his ideals for good governance skillfully in the following quotation:

> In the best of all worlds, it is a coalition of the board, the governor, the legislative leaders, a community group, the chancellors, and the presidents. Because there is such a diversity among states and state universities...diverse forces have brought forward the needed aspiration to quality. Part of the difficulty in creating a powerful aspiration for having universities of high quality is that it is tied to the broader issue of the state's self image. (Newman, 1987, p. 91)

Following the work by both Newman and Hines, other researchers began to take a look at specific states and the structural effectiveness of their higher education governance systems. In Louisiana, Dugas employed a stepwise regression model to predict levels of support for higher education among members of the legislature (Dugas, 1994). Shugar's investigation of the relationship between public higher education governance systems and the perceptions of high-echelon administrators utilized a survey instrument across seven Midwestern states to determine the governance structure perceived to achieve maximum effectiveness within public institutions of higher education (Shugar, 1994). Shugar's investigation led him to conclude that administrators across seven Midwestern states were "seeking a more simplified governance structure with more control at the local level" (Shugar, 1994, p. 116). A governance structure emphasizing simplicity and local control was viewed as the optimum operational structure available, according to Shugar's study; particularly one that averted unwelcomed infringement on academic programs and areas of "academic activity that should reside within the local control of the institution" (Shugar, p. 136).

Other dissertations have made significant contributions. In Mississippi, Heindle's study examined the relationship between the Mississippi legislature and public institutions of higher learning during a twenty-five-year period (Heindle, 1993). Balogh concluded in her ninety-year historical study that the use of citizen boards appeared to discourage some types of legislative intrusion (Balogh, 1993).

Louisiana was the site of an historical study by Brown on the impact of politics on governance (Brown, 1993). Brown's study is particularly interesting because it takes a look at a decentralized coordinating-board state in a similar manner as this research. Brown's dissertation entitled "Governance of Higher Education in Louisiana: The Process and Impact of Politics" featured a heavy concentration on historical analysis (Brown, 1993). Traditional secondary research sources were supplemented with some personal interviews (Brown, 1993, p. 30). Although short on substantive policy information and recommendations, Brown's work provided documentation regarding the autonomous relationship between the Louisiana state government and its heavily decentralized university system using a multiple-board format. Her research can be viewed as a reference point for this case study, but it should be noted that the purposes and method for each differed significantly. Brown's catechization focused on two components: development of a documentation of the history of Louisiana's governance structure and understanding why Louisiana's structure was so strongly autonomous. As a logical next step to the work of Brown, the research in this document explores whether Maine's unified governance mechanism responds to the political will of state government under a much different set of variables. Although some may view this as a very fine difference, the focal point of this study is nevertheless vastly different from that of Brown, and the two studies should not be considered replicative.

For example, Brown noted that "The politicians who argue most to change the structure to a single-board system focus on the inefficiencies and wastefulness of the current system, yet there is little substance to their argument other than general dissatisfaction" (Brown, 1993, p. 190). As will be seen later in this research, the wastefulness and inefficiency argument cited in the Louisiana system was similar to documented reasoning used to justify the creation of the University of Maine System. Readers that refer to her work should note differences between the consolidated, segmental Louisiana system established in 1974 and the unified governing approach established in Maine in 1968. Rather than examining a unified system of governance with one governing board as in this Maine-based research, Brown examined a structure in Louisiana that was nearly opposite in terms of its legal underpinnings. Generally,

2: Literature Review

Louisiana's governance structure is referred to as a multi-campus, segmental system, and it consists of coordinating-board oversight with multiple, campus-based regulatory boards (McGuinness, 1994, p. 11). Brown's study correctly noted that the Louisiana governance structure was resilient to change due at least in part to the fact that the structure was incorporated into the state constitution (Brown, 1993, p. 176). In Maine, no constitutional provisions exist, and any attempt at isolating the constitutional variable should be viewed with an eye toward understanding the additional impact of state constitutional law.

The following passage from Brown's conclusion supports the importance of a divergence between the examination of state systems that have differences such as constitutional mandates and the examination of those that do not:

> In this study, the autonomous status of the governance structure emerged as being more influential in the persistence of the structure, as opposed to the influence of a governor or legislature...there was little evidence of the process of accommodation to environmental stress. (Brown, 1993, p. 187)

As we prepare to examine the state of Maine, our eye needs to be focused on whether accommodation to environmental stress exists in a system that has no constitutional provisions.

Another recent major study of note was prepared for and copyrighted by the California Higher Education Policy Center in 1997. "State Structures for the Governance of Higher Education: A Comparative Study" was compiled to relate "the organization of state higher education systems to the achievement of state policy objectives" (Bowen, Bracco, Callan, Finney, Richardson, & Trombley, 1997, p. 1, Executive Summary). Seven state systems were examined in detail via case-study analyses in an attempt to document systems and later to compare system performance. In addressing the issue of performance differences among state systems of higher education relative to their choice of governance structure, one California Higher Education Policy Center analysis revealed the following:

Our research suggests that differences in governance structures do influence the performance of higher education systems, including system responsiveness to state priorities. Elected leaders in Illinois, Texas, Georgia, and Florida identify and communicate priorities to their higher education systems. Not surprisingly, these systems are perceived to be more responsive than those in New York and Michigan, where elected leaders rely primarily on market influences and the budget to shape institutional priorities. In Florida, the absence of balanced attention to institutional and professional values contributes to stalling and other forms of subsystem resistance to legislatively determined priorities. Both the absence of market influences and a thirty-six-year-old master plan that insulates public subsystems from each other and from state government produce a system in California that is notably non-responsive to external influences. (Bowen, et al., pp. 4-5, The Research Questions Answered)

The Policy Center's research suggested that "differences in governance structures do influence the performance of higher education systems" (Bowen, et al., 1997, p. 1, Executive Summary). One of the most important questions identified was "whether the system exhibits the capacity to recognize and respond in some organized and efficient way to state needs and contextual changes" (Bowen, et al., 1997, p. 1, Executive Summary).

Maine's capacity to respond is examined in following chapters, but it is safe to remark here that the characteristics of responsiveness of some states to external influences compare in interesting ways. The national literature reflects a possible causal link between resulting behaviors that some states have exhibited over the years and the specific nature of their structural properties.

Part Two: The Maine System

Historical Development

Things could have been much different for Maine. For example, there was discussion in the formative years as to whether Maine's new system for higher education should be constitutionally based or statutorily based. Eventually, a statutorily based system was favored, following a great deal of debate about the differences between the two options. Part 2 of this chapter will examine the history, theory, and actions behind the governance decisions made in the state of Maine.

Prior to the reorganization of Maine public higher education in 1968, concern ran high among educators, the press, legislators, and citizens that public institutions were suffering from a lack of coordination and cooperation. As a result, critics believed that academic quality suffered in contrast to other states. A movement began in the late 1950s and early 1960s to reexamine the state of affairs in public higher education to discover whether there really was a problem and, if so, what should be done about it.

This movement came to a head with the Higher Education Facilities Act of 1963 and the Advisory Commission for the Higher Education Study that it created. One of the early acts of this Commission was to hire a well-known national nonprofit corporation to conduct a comprehensive review of higher education delivery in the state of Maine and, based on their study, present recommendations for improvement. The nonprofit corporation was known as the Academy for Educational Development, Incorporated, and their recommendations were intended to form the basis for a master plan for higher education in Maine. This document, called "The First Business of Our Times," was completed by September of 1966. The name of the report was taken from a quotation by Maine's Governor Reed, who stressed that "education actually is the first business of our times" (State of Maine, 1966, Letter of Transmittal).

In 1966, there was no University of Maine System. Maine public higher education functioned through a series of campuses scattered throughout the state. The dominant force was the University of Maine, with campuses in Orono and Portland. The University of Maine was the land-grant institution of the state, and as such offered most of the programs that were not based in teacher or vocational education. It offered the majority of the master's degree programs and all of the Ph.D. programs. An eleven-member board of directors controlled the campus.

The University of Maine was joined by the Maine Maritime Academy as an institution with its own board. Maine Maritime maintained a twelve-member board of directors to coordinate the state's merchant marine program (State of Maine, 1966, p. 18).

The State Board of Education governed the remaining public institutions in the state. These institutions were divided between vocational-technical institutes and state colleges. The vocational institutions were located in Auburn, Bangor, Presque Isle, and South Portland; the state colleges were located in Fort Kent, Gorham, Machias, Farmington, and Presque Isle. For the most part, the state colleges originated as teachers colleges and concentrated their offerings in kindergarten through secondary school teacher-training, with some authority to expand into other liberal arts offerings (State of Maine, 1966, p.18).

"The First Business of Our Times" report was the strongest and most comprehensive look at higher education to date, with the previous examination of the environment of Maine's higher education having been completed during the 1920s. The Academy for Educational Development was well versed on trends and management in other states, and by the date of its report, the group was convinced that Maine had a problem that needed attention. The focus was on areas of control, coordination and state administration.

For example, each campus had a separate line item in the state budget. That meant that campuses competed against each other for state resources, a practice frowned upon by academics and government leaders in other states. In addition, program decisions made at the land-grant campus were separate from the other state campuses, with little or no opportunity taken to evaluate duplication of effort or strategize or coordinate offerings. There were many management and business functions required in running higher education institutions that, if consolidated, could potentially lead to economies of scale. With the rate of attainment of post-secondary degrees among Maine youths playing an important role in the debate, the Academy for Educational Development presented a bold new approach to the Advisory Committee and the Legislature that sought to bring all of the state liberal arts institutions under an umbrella University of Maine System.

A close reading of the Academy's recommendations reveals a detectable bias toward establishment of a master plan for the public institutions of higher education in the state. In reviewing the section of the report on public policy for higher education, there develops a stark but familiar realization that while most in higher education circles would prefer state governments to outline the necessity of higher education in their constitutions, the process to achieve such a result is difficult. The political reality in Maine at the time was that not only was education absent in the state constitution, it also was purposely absent. The issue of local control in education and other matters left legislatures around the country with little appetite to make changes of the magnitude of an amendment to their constitutions. A two-thirds legislative vote requirement combined with gubernatorial and voter approval made such a recommendation unwise in Maine.

The next best alternative to supporters of higher education was to set up public policy in such a way as to require a master plan. The Academy was clearly an advocate for higher education and could not be considered an impartial investigator, as evidenced by their opening salvo: "The Academy seeks the opportunity to work on projects that lead to action in improving educational programs and practices" (State of Maine, 1966, p. i). Nevertheless, the master plan supported by The Academy had the advantage of requiring simple statutory change by majority vote of the legislature and signature by the governor. Not only did a master plan feature the benefits of coordination and control with an eye toward the future, the plan also contained within it accompanying structural changes that insulated higher education from outside pressures. This reasoning was reflected in the words from "The First Business of Our Times" report. Notice how the Academy progressed from the constitutional framework into a master plan arrangement:

> Few state constitutions in this country were written, or have been rewritten or amended, to recognize the importance of, or the public's responsibility for, providing higher education... Rarely have the various acts and orders been codified or reevaluated as they relate to higher education.
>
> A higher education master plan should function as a detailed description of public policy. The plan...should give the people the assurance that their state is interested in, indeed committed to, the furtherance of higher education opportunities for all its citizens. (State of Maine, 1966, p.14)

This part of the report was reflective of a national train of thought that espoused master plans as the clear alternative to constitutional provisions.

2: Literature Review

Embedded within these recommendations was a new structure with a unified or umbrella board of trustees who would serve to make all campus resource allocation decisions. The elimination of the line items in favor of a block grant from the state's general fund to trustees presented the opportunity for a major policy shift toward academic independence-if not at the campus level, at least at the level of the board of trustees. Insulation from some forms of legislative interference in the workings of public institutions of higher education was a feature that appealed to educational administrators. Finally, in 1968, the new system came to pass.

In the beginning, the new system was not as clearly defined as it is today. Fort Kent, Aroostook, Washington, Farmington, and Gorham began their tenure as state colleges and Orono, Bangor, Augusta, Portland, and the Law School in Portland began as universities. This arrangement changed quickly with the merger of Portland and Gorham into the University of Maine Portland/Gorham, later called the University of Southern Maine, and the reconfiguration of campuses that is described in the upcoming discussion.

According to both law and tradition in Maine, the Board of Trustees has the ultimate responsibility for decision-making. Following the centralization of the structure in 1968, the Board's role was firmly established. A description of that role appeared in the 1972 report, "Higher Education Planning for Maine":

> The University of Maine exists as a corporation chartered by the State of Maine. Thus it has a private character as well as a public responsibility. The Board of Trustees should continue to have full and final responsibility for and authority over the governance of the University of Maine as required by law. The primary responsibility of the Board of Trustees should be to ensure the long-run welfare of the University and to support the University in its relationships with other agencies and with its external constituencies. The channel of authority from the Board of Trustees to the University community should continue to be through the Chancellor. Under the law the Chancellor is the "chief administrative and education officer" of the University of Maine. He [sic: The Chancellor] should exercise complete administrative authority over the institutions comprising the

2: Literature Review

University of Maine, subject to the advice, approval, and control of the Board of Trustees. He [sic: The Chancellor] should share this authority with the heads of the campuses in appropriate and significant ways, as decisions are reached which affect the campuses. He [sic: The Chancellor] should recognize the need for autonomy on each campus. (Higher Education Planning Commission, 1972, p. 99)

This strong governance statement would appear to have established the Board of Trustees with the kind of buffer between the university and government so often desired by academia.

At some of the early board meetings, votes were taken that shaped the unified structure. In the System's infancy, many actions were carried out as a result of the legislative dictate or from public reports resulting from the original consolidation. For example, at the Board of Trustees meeting in Bangor on December 18, 1969, the following action was taken:

Voted: That as of July 1970, the University of Maine in Portland as the School of Law be detached from the jurisdiction of the Orono Campus and consolidated with Gorham State College as a new unit of the University of Maine, which shall be called the University of Maine, Portland-Gorham. (Board of Trustees of the University of Maine System, 1969, December 18, p. 2)

The location of the Law School in Portland made it ideally suited to become a part of the University of Southern Maine for geographic, demographic, and administrative reasons. Chancellor McNeil, the System's first chancellor, was given the authority by the Board to lead the reorganization of the law school on its behalf.

Not all decisions that were made in the System's infancy were as effective. For example, most onlookers have viewed Maine's handling of the statewide community-college system operating under the umbrella of the University of Maine System as a failure. At the same December 1969 trustees meeting in which the Law school decision was made, the following motion established the community college concept: "Voted:

2: Literature Review

That the Bangor and Augusta campuses be developed as the first units of a community college system within the University" (Board of Trustees of the University of Maine System, 1969, December 18, p. 2). This vote appeared to be a good start toward offering the benefits of higher education to a specific segment of the market. The Bangor and Augusta campuses still function today. But the growth of the system would be haphazard, as campuses like Augusta were allowed to become four-year, degree-granting institutions without significantly revamping the community-college component.

A part of the System that experienced successful growth and development was Educational Television (ETV). Television was a part of the System since its formation. The television component later became the Maine Public Broadcasting Network as a result of a motion made on September 28, 1970 (Board of Trustees of the University of Maine System, 1970, September 28, p. 6). Two years later, on November 9, 1972, at Portland, it was voted "to authorize the submission of a separate appropriation request to the Governor and the 106th Legislature for the Maine Public Broadcasting Network" (Board of Trustees of the University of Maine System, 1972, November 9, p. 4). Eventually, the Maine Public Broadcasting Network continued its affiliation with the University of Maine System but would establish its own trustees and make its own decisions.

Over the course of the 1970s and 1980s, the legal buffer between the state and the university system grew wider. For example, after much study and debate, a statement of the public policy on higher education was added to the Maine statutes. These principles were strong endorsements for independence, and included the following statements codified into law as of 1984 (partial list):

...3. Cohesive System. To develop, maintain, and support a structure of public higher education in the State which will assure the most cohesive system possible for planning, action, and service in providing higher educational opportunities, to which the highest priority for fiscal support shall be assigned...

5. Encourage Growth. To encourage the growth and development of existing or new private higher educational institutions within the State where studies justify their continuation or establishment;

6. All Citizens Eligible. To recognize that all citizens shall be considered eligible for the benefits of appropriate higher education, whether they are high school graduates or the equivalent, or those seeking retraining or training for new careers;

7. Public Funds. To assign continually a high priority in the allocation of public funds to the development of services, programs, and institutions designed to provide opportunities for those who do not now share equitably in the advantages of higher education, because of limiting economic, social, educational, and cultural factors;

8. Financial Support. To support financially the programs of public higher educational institutions through appropriations, grants, and loans, based on comprehensive lans [sic: loans] and budgets, both short-term and long-term;

9. Public Accountability. To expect appropriate public accountability for this support;

10. Federal Funds. To encourage all institutions, public and private, to make maximum use of federal funds available for the support of higher educational programs and activities, the State to provide matching funds, where necessary, initially and on a continuing basis;

11. Cooperative Undertakings. To expect and request cooperative undertakings among the higher educational institutions, public and private, and between them and the business, industrial and labor interests, to further the development of quality and quantity in educational programs and services and the advancement of the state's economy;

12. Evaluation and Research. To encourage a continuing program of evaluation and research with respect to higher educational opportunities in the State through financial support and the expectation of annual reporting;

13. Master Plan. To give a high priority to the provisions of the master plan for higher education through legislative action and appropriate publicity;

14. Commuter Education. To make the most effective use possible of the financial resources allocated to public higher education by maximum emphasis on commuter facilities;

15. Transfer of Credits. To provide for a uniform system of transferring credits for equivalent courses between the various units of the University of Maine. (Wilson, 1985, pp. 108-109)

Within many states, similar tenets are found, but the legal means for the organizational structure differs greatly across the state boundaries, particularly when constitutional provisions exist. An examination of each state's underpinnings revealed that the variety of differences often hinged on variations in the level of autonomy granted to campuses and systems, as well as emerging or continuing levels of government involvement. An important future consideration in this research will be the examination of whether or not the state of Maine has carried out that which has been codified into law, including the measures listed here.

Current Structure

Thirty-two years of change has brought a few more statutes regarding the governance of Maine higher education, but no overarching constitutional provision or other major change. University governance in Maine is still shared, however equally or unequally, among the University System, the executive branch, and the legislative branch of government, until and unless the judicial branch is called upon for a ruling. In all fifty states, Washington, D.C., and Puerto Rico, the same is true to a greater or lesser degree, despite many different forms of organizational hierarchy and governance. Restructuring has changed the face of some of these systems. In Maine, shifts in the basic organizational structure (Figure 2.1, following) have not occurred.

Many of the chancellors, presidents and trustees have maintained that the State's current structure of higher education, as defined by 20-A, Chapter 409, 411, and 431-A of the Maine Revised Statutes, provides a level of institutional autonomy that is paramount to the effective governance of higher education. Others have argued that the structure gives too much autonomy to the trustees. Still others would like to see a decentralized or coordinated system patterned after other states with powerful campus-based approaches. As a result of the call for

2: Literature Review

decentralization, Maine recently installed visiting committees at each campus. As will be discussed later, these boards have thus far been largely ceremonial in nature, but their function and role is sure to evolve over time. In essence, the figure presented here represents the University of Maine System's likeness since 1968. Campus names have changed and some reorganization has occurred, but the unified nature of the structure has persevered.

The following figure examines the current University of Maine structure:

THE UNIVERSITY OF MAINE GOVERNANCE STRUCTURE

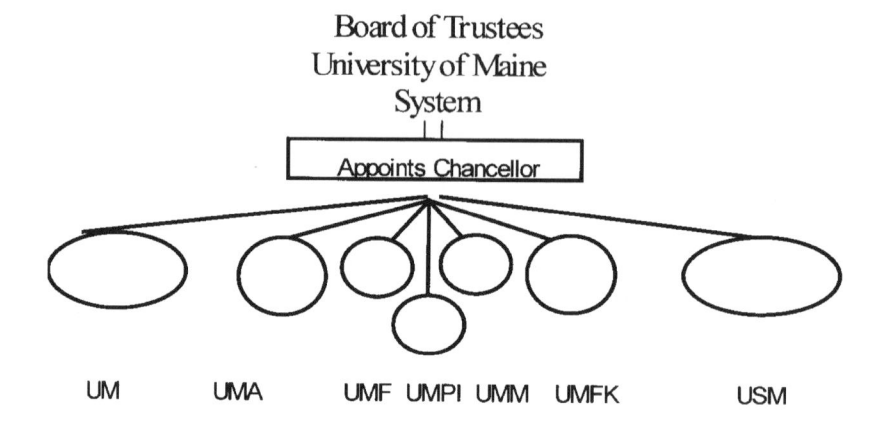

Board of Trustees
University of Maine
System

Appoints Chancellor

UM   UMA   UMF UMPI UMM UMFK   USM

Key:
Left to right: University of Maine; University of Maine at Augusta; at Farmingtion; at Presque Isle; at Machias; at Fort Kent; University of Southern Maine

Figure 2.1: The Consolidated Governing Board Structure of the Maine System

The Maine State Legislature created the University of Maine System in 1968. It currently consists of seven campuses, with the Orono location designated as the flagship campus. This designation is based on its historical foundation as a Land Grant and Sea Grant institution. Other campuses are located in Fort Kent, Presque Isle, Machias, Farmington,

2: Literature Review

Augusta/Bangor, and Portland/Gorham/Lewiston. Within this campus system there are outreach programs, cooperative extensions, and other programs, including a recently controversial but advancing educational network for distance learning.

A sixteen-member Board of Trustees governs the system. The Governor nominates all trustees, with the exception of the student member, for five-year terms, with one allowable term of reappointment. The student representative may serve a single two-year term. The Maine Legislature's Joint Standing Committee on Education and Cultural Affairs conducts a hearing for each nominee, and the Maine Senate confirms the nomination.

The Board of Trustees is the executive body of the entire System. The Board appoints a system chancellor, who is responsible for academic and administrative functions. No chancellor can act without the delegation of authority by the Board. The Board also reviews the chancellor's performance, appoints campus presidents, establishes programmatic changes, sets tuition rates, and finalizes all operating budgets and other related matters.

Given the evidence about the organizational component of the University of Maine System and the laws that are in place, what role, then, does the Governor of Maine have in the establishment of a future direction for higher education? How does the Governor's role compare to chancellors, legislators, and board members? In the following analysis of Maine governors and chancellors since 1968 and their impact on higher education, these roles begin to define themselves.

CHAPTER THREE: RESEARCH PROBLEM AND METHOD

> *The challenge of post-secondary organizational theory and research is to try to understand what holds together these fascinating institutions as organizations and what makes them more effective.*
>
> Marvin W. Peterson
> From: "Emerging Developments in Postsecondary Organization Theory and Research: Fragmentation or Integration," in *Educational Researcher*, Volume 14, Issue 3, March 1985

Conceptual Framework

States and their university systems need each other to function. The more that can be known about this relationship, the better the state and university policy that will be written. This simple premise provides the framework to begin the analytical process. The goal of this research was to thoroughly examine historical, legal, and perceptual artifacts over the entire life span of a unified state university system in order to effectively explore its attributes and its ability to function in coexistence with external forces, particularly state governments.

Of all of the various state structures in use today, the unified system of university governance can be said to be the most centralized because it is composed of a single board of overseers responsible for the operations of all campuses in the system. It allows many decisions to be made at the trustee level in conjunction with the recommendation of a chancellor, for example. The unified system is also thought to be a very independent form of university governance, in that final decisions are generally made by appointed trustees, other than an allocation of a block amount of appropriations by state government. In Maine, one independent governing board retains authority over the entire system.

The state of Maine decided to charter the unified mechanism to govern the University of Maine System in 1968. Despite many attempts to change or even dismantle it, the University of Maine System still retains its original statutory character. It continues to be exposed to the potential for major government intervention, as is true of many other states to a greater or lesser degree. That is why this research undertook a penetrating look at the precise manner in which the University of Maine System's design negotiates external intrusion and legislative and executive branch interventions.

Subject Matter and Scope

This book takes the form of a case study examining the terms of the relationship between state government in Maine and the higher education bureaucracy that it established. The State of Maine's role in assuring efficient and effective operations in a unified system of governance was critically explored. Maine's governance responsibility was contrasted with the ability of its university system to plot a direction of its own within the unified format of governance. Maine was chosen for this project because no prior examination of its history and origins exists. It is a system that has encountered unique problems during a period of many years. These problems fluctuated in severity. There were times when some of Maine's citizenry went so far as to call for the elimination of the entire system of organization itself.

The University of Maine System is an ideal size for a project of this scope in terms of its number of campuses, its programs, and even its major players. Maine is a small state of 1.3 million residents, and it has a small number of students relative to systems such as in North Carolina, Michigan, Florida, and New York, to name just a few. Its age of approximately thirty-two years make its existence short enough to fully document, but long enough to consider its life cycle. Finally, a variety of historically challenging political battles and various attempts to change or eliminate the unified structure made it a nearly perfect breeding ground for a content analysis.

General questions that were addressed by solid evidence from this research included: What can be learned about the political environment for decision-making through a legal, historical, and structural analysis of a unified system? Which issues in Maine best displayed the interplay between structure and the external environment? How does Maine's unified governance structure react to outside interventions?

Little research has been done nationally that examines the political effectiveness of specific agency structures for higher education, but thanks to national policy centers, some studies, and a few unique dissertations, this void is slowly being filled. A representation of the national research is referenced in this document.

The notion that each state's method of governance was developed over time and is based on its own needs confound the analysis. As a result, some researchers may have been kept at an arm's length from the subject matter. There is research available, but results are inconclusive as to which method of governance promotes or inhibits university growth, or which structure most effectively encourages or resists outside interventions, for example. The potential to explore current systems of governance for higher education are nearly limitless. For example, public universities may be operating within a legal or constitutional framework or very little framework at all. They may run on "auto pilot" or they may require strong institutional leadership. There may be complex "Webberian" system bureaucracies or tremendous campus autonomies. By continuing to refine the exploratory process, the states may learn more about what has worked under certain circumstances and what has not. The research contained in this book presupposes that with the help of a methodological construct, a comprehensive look at the record of a single university system will lead to a better understanding of the reason for its current condition. More importantly, new knowledge may lead to a circumstance in which policymakers have a better ability to shape systems that can adhere to the predefined aims of its creators and/or to the goals and needs of today's citizens.

Research Design

With the axiom of ever-increasing levels of external influence on public systems of higher education firmly established in the academic literature, this study began by trying to find new and better ways of documenting, measuring, and analyzing this phenomenon. With a study question and goals in hand, the process of an exhaustive collection and review of national and state literature was undertaken. Thousands of documents over a period stretching from about 1960 to 2000 were analyzed. The data are described in Table 3.1.

Several elements of governance were discovered during the initial fact-finding work that led to documentation of questions needing critical exploration. Examples of areas that were considered for exploration in this study include such topics as the impact of legally imposed decision-

30   *3: Research Problem and Method*

making limits on unified structures, the potential effect of adding constitutional provisions to a unified system, and the effectiveness of shared governance principles under unified structures. While these topics are discussed in this document, they were not chosen as the focal point of the study. Clearly, they deserve further exploration elsewhere.

Evidence from exploration of this secondary data revealed that Maine's specialized agency structure would provide a good testing ground for a content analysis about the nature and level of various political or government interventions into policy outcomes that are normally reserved for trustees under a unified agency structure format. For the purposes of this research, content analysis was defined by Holsti as a "technique for making inferences by systematically and objectively identifying specified characteristics of messages" (Lindzey, 1968, p. 601).

An important early consideration was the determination of the rules of this content analysis that would best lead to an examination of all materials, and not just materials that might support an investigator's specific hypothesis.

In preparation of this, the work of Yin was consulted and determined to be appropriate for design and utilization under these research conditions. In Yin's *Case Study Research*, four major designs are discussed (Yin, 1994, p. 38). These designs are represented by the following depiction:

CASE-STUDY DESIGNS

single-case designs　　　　　　　　　　　　multiple-case designs

Type 1: holistic single unit of analysis	Type 3: holistic single unit of analysis
Type 2: embedded multiple units of analysis	Type 4: embedded multiple units of analysis

Figure 3.1 Basic Types of Designs for Case Studies
Source: COSMOS Corporation (Yin, 1994, p. 39)

In terms of design, a study of the level of government intervention into decision-making at the University of Maine System represents a single-case analysis, so multiple-case designs represented by Type 3 and Type 4 did not apply. The relevant question in this case analysis was whether the study would be of a holistic or embedded nature. According to Yin, case studies may contain analyses that give attention to a sub-unit or sub-units (Yin, 1994, p. 41). When specific scientific analyses of sub-units are involved, the research is an embedded case-study design; when the case study examines the global nature of an organization, it is known to be holistic (Yin, p. 42).

The research conducted in this case included multiple sources of information on several units within the University of Maine System; therefore, the embedded single-case-study design was chosen with the hope of building a rich and diverse range of evidence that would lead to the ability of any researcher to replicate findings.

Table 3.1, located at the end of this chapter, describes the kinds of data collected for each investigated circumstance. The wide variety of data and the inferences from these sources are categorized in the table to explain how this investigation was conducted.

Developing the Research Questions

The role of government in higher education is constantly evolving. This study asserts that one good way to examine the phenomenon is through a case-by-case, state-by-state analysis. If each state is examined individually, governance structures can be compared and similarities and nuances that develop during political encounters can be effectively captured.

Consider the progression of the following statements (and many others just like them), forwarded by well-respected commissions/authors at the top of their profession. Similar statements can be found in studies, position papers, textbooks, and pronouncements too numerous to mention here, but these are generally indicative of the body of literature from the field. Two sets of statements are examined. The first group begins in 1971 with a recognition that government interventions may have more impact in unified systems. Notice the progression of the observations within the first five statements. There is a perceptible shift in the focus of these researchers/practitioners from acknowledging and resisting unwanted government interventions into university operations, toward understanding them and working within them. These statements

3: Research Problem and Method

are broad and, with the exception of Lee and Bowen, they refer to all types of university organization.

Contemplating the first set, we have:

(1) *1971*
Lee and Bowen in *The Multicampus University*:
> The multicampus system is more open to control by external authority, particularly by governors, than would be a series of separate board campuses. Among other reasons, a governor can be effective on one board in a way he [sic: or she] could not be on ten or twenty or fifty campus boards. (Lee and Bowen, 1971, p. xiv)

(2) *1973*
The Carnegie Commission in its *Governance of Higher Education Report*:
> External authorities are exercising more and more authority over higher education, and institutional independence has been declining. The greatest shift of power in recent years has taken place not inside the campus, but in the transfer of authority from the campus to outside agencies. (Carnegie Commission, 1973, p. 1)

(3) *1980*
W. H. Cowely in *Presidents, Professors, and Trustees*:
> Many in academe today are appalled by the forceful role played by the federal and state governments in the affairs of higher education. This role strikes academics as in-appropriate and out of keeping with the historic autonomy which they believe higher education has heretofore enjoyed in its relations with civil government. A closer look at that history will show, however, that civil government has long played a role in the affairs of colleges and universities. (Cowley, 1980, p. 186)

(4) 1980
Frank Newman in *Choosing Quality*:
At the outset of this project, we held a somewhat simpler view of the state/university relationship-namely, that there is a tendency for states to intrude in the affairs of state universities and a need on the universities' part for greater autonomy. As we studied the issues, we found that the relationship is more complex. There is indeed a tendency for states to intrude and, in fact, for the universities to cause or invite that intrusion. (Newman, 1980, prologue)

(5) 1998
Terrence MacTaggart in *Seeking Excellence Through Independence*:
As legislators demanded to know more about and to control the destiny of the higher education systems they funded, the central offices of those systems themselves became more active in regulating campus academic and financial policy....The dialectic between the organs of state government on the one hand and system offices on the other meant that increasingly the power to make decisions on what programs to offer and how much to spend on them resided with the system, not the campus. (MacTaggart, 1998, p. 5)

These statements go beyond simply pointing out that state governments play a role in the governance of the university systems for which they provide funds. They show a perceptible progression toward the realization among university administrators, chief executives, chancellors, and other leaders that government will be involved either to a greater or lesser extent. In the case of the final statement in the first set, there is an open admission that, at the very least, the potential for government involvement may lead to the usurping of campus decisions from presidents to chancellors. With this understanding, we can begin to formulate the research questions. First, there is another strand of thought in the literature that, due to its prominence, needed to be examined.

The understanding of the need to govern state university systems within an interactive environment is not a new paradigm by any means.

Despite the perceived increases in intervention attempts, relatively few writers have depicted the clash between the forces of government and the university. The following paragraphs provide examples of a solid understanding of the relationship throughout the second half of this century:

(1) *1965*
David Easton in *A Framework for Political Analysis*:
Persistence of patterns of interaction capable of meeting the fundamental political functions require that the members engaging in this activity be able to adapt, correct, readjust, control, or modify the system or its parameters to cope with the problems created by internal or external stress. (Easton, 1965, p. 80)

(2) *1980*
Frank Newman in *Choosing Quality*:
What becomes clear is that the real need is not simply for more autonomy but for a relationship between the university and the state that is constructive for both, built up over a long period of time by careful attention on the part of all parties. (Newman, 1980, Prologue)

(3) *1995*
Aims C. McGuinness, Jr., in *The Changing Structure of State Higher Education Leadership:*
From the perspective of colleges and universities, the board should serve as a buffer against inappropriate external intrusion and should advocate the needs of higher education to the state and the broader society. From the perspective of the public and the state political leadership, the board should transmit the priorities of the broader society to the academy, be a force for change and a protector of the broader public interest. In the best of times, the role is to be a constructive, mediating force between contradictory perspectives. But in more times than not, it is to be vilified by one side or the other,

occasionally ignored altogether, and sometimes crushed in the middle. (National Center for Higher Education Management Systems, 1995, p. 6)

(4) *1998*
Peterson and McLendon in *Seeking Excellence Through Independence*:
There is a continuous conflict between institutional concern for maintaining autonomy and the state's press for accountability and control. State coordination is expressed in constant struggles over legislation and appropriations issues and the ongoing legal battles between the state and its institutions to clarify their constitutional autonomy. Maintaining an appropriate level of institutional cooperation and statewide coordination in the midst of a competitive and occasionally conflictual environment is a dynamic system requiring continuous attention by institutions and state leaders. (MacTaggart, 1998, pp. 172-173)

To over-generalize based on these statements would be unwise, given the profound and complex differences between the states and their governance structures. Nevertheless, an emerging theme from academic leaders in the national literature appears to be that the governance of the university might best be accomplished through structural mechanisms and personal leadership that fosters independence while allowing for state level accountability. Apart from personal leadership, which system or structure best promotes such an outcome?

A few states have moved forward with reorganization in an approach that both displays state government's ultimate power over the process and, at the same time, hands the reigns of governance back to the university. New Jersey, which has experienced several major reforms accomplished partly through the efforts of Governor Christine Todd Whitman, moved forward with a new form of decentralized accountability. This closely watched phenomenon was described by Greer in *Seeking Excellence Through Independence* (MacTaggart, 1998). Greer points out that a few states are changing relationships between their state government and the structure of governance responsible for higher education:

> New Jersey...has achieved a significant amount of autonomy from state government since the mid-1980s....The New Jersey experience with institutional self-governance evolves from an explicit public policy decision to provide institutions with greater autonomy over their affairs... (MacTaggart, 1998, p. 84).

The key policy principle driving the autonomy movement and restructuring law asserts that quality, educational service, innovation, and accountability are more likely to be upheld through policy set by local boards of trustees rather than through a centralized state bureaucracy (MacTaggart, 1998, p. 84).

New Jersey held to four principles in its reorganization effort:
- Higher education must be affordable, accessible, and of high quality.
- Institutions require greater autonomy with a minimum of bureaucratic controls.
- The new structure must guard against political intrusion.
- Appropriate coordination should be provided by the state and the institutions themselves (MacTaggart, 1998, p. 84).

The analysis of these principles and others like them permeates discussion about systems research across the country. If state governments are to demand reorganization due to a set of vague factors relating to accountability, it appears that many in academia would like to pursue approaches that strengthen decentralization over bureaucratic state coordinating boards and/or that improve the decision-making power of system presidents. While this is a rational position for a president to take, faculty yearn for the principles of shared governance to help screen intrusive board or government meddling into internal affairs, such as curriculum changes, distance-learning strategies, tuition levels, and many other university matters. Legislators demand responsiveness and are distrustful of the system in many cases. Chancellors feel the pressure to centralize operations. What factors can help guide university leaders and state governments to make the right decisions in their unique situations?

Primary Research Questions and Propositions

This book is not designed to answer the many questions that plague the government/university relationship on a national scale. It is instead designed to examine the question of political or governmental intervention as it relates to governance in a state using the unified-governance mechanism. The research design makes the assumption that the road to continuous improvement lies within what can be learned from state-specific content analysis. As a result, the following specific questions were formulated to direct the course of this investigation:

(1) Are state government interventions taking place within Maine's unified system of governance?

(2) If yes, what kind of interventions are taking place? How and why do they occur?

(3) Does the unified-governance system allow for effective interaction between internal university governance and external state involvement? How so?

(4) What are some of the resolved and unresolved issues within the University of Maine System that support and/or do not support the unified structure as a model for governance in the age of increasing government interventions?

According to Yin, one rationale for using the single-case study design method takes place when a critical case tests a well-formulated theory (Yin, 1994, p. 38). In this book, the theory that was formalized is set forth in the following proposition: that unified-agency structures, designed by law for the delivery of a multi-campus system of higher education, are measurably responsive to increasing levels of government interventions.

This proposition is simpler to evaluate than one based on a more complex theory of state/university interactive relationships. For the purposes of this study, a crucial first step was anthropological in nature: the identification of events where strong interventions were attempted by political entities, such as governors, legislators, and/or others. Only after relevant interventions were found and their effects carefully traced was the University of Maine System's responsiveness (i.e., how flexible: resiliency vs. pliancy) to these interventions evaluated.

The Political Interventions Model

The model represented in Table 3.1 following this section was used to evaluate the proposition, or hypothesis. In the left-hand column, the physical units within the University of Maine System are identified. These include the System itself and its components, such as the land-grant institution, other campuses, interactive television (UNET), and community college offerings. Each data source was analyzed through the actions, behaviors, and opinions of intermediate units (in this case, trustees, chancellors, legislators, and governors, for example). Raw data sources such as speeches, studies, plans, hearings, and the like (represented in the top half of the model) were cross-referenced to gain insight on political interventions and other managerial issues confronting the University of Maine System.

Major political interventions were identified by tracking specific events and policy behavior expressed by the presiding trustees and the chancellor when confronted by political pressures. Reactions to each major political intervention were documented; from this, the impact of the intervention was evaluated. For example, when confronted about the University System's investments in South Africa during apartheid, what was the university response? Which forces played a role in the response? Why? What can be learned about the unified structure's ability to cope with the intervention? These questions are addressed and conclusions are drawn.

Alternatively, the data also provided information about the University System's ability to resist intervention attempts. What impact might this independence have on future attempts to intervene? What is the impact on public-policy formulation? These questions are addressed beginning in Chapter 5. Through this manner of careful triangulation, a sense was also developed about whether the System has met the expectations of its founders as it is written in the founding reports and in statutes. These issues are discussed in Chapter 6.

As can be seen by the following evaluative model in Table 3.1, the reported views, beliefs, and values of many prominent figures were combined with documentation of the actual political events as they occurred to form the basis of the findings of this research. This model is new but is based on the work of Holsti and Yin, and it will hereafter be referred to as the "political intervention identification model." Following

3: Research Problem and Method 39

the model's data organization, Table 3.2 provides a close look at the major reports about the University of Maine System compiled over the years. This table provides a reference for researchers who wish to take a closer look at the development of the System. Each report played a major role in the development of this research.

Organization of Data Sources for Case Study

Units	Total System Data Source:	Trustees Data Source:	Chancellors Data Source:	Governors Data Source:	Presidents Data Source:	Campus Faculty Data Source:	Students Data Source:	Legislators Data Source:	Others Data Source:
	Minutes Records Plans Reports Budgets Studies Newspapers Policy Manuals Journals	Minutes Records Plans Reports Budgets Studies Newspapers Policy Manuals Journals	Speeches Manuscripts Books Personal communication Records Minutes Plans Reports Budgets Studies Newspapers Policy Manuals Journals	Campaigns Proposals Books Speeches Reports Budgets Newspapers Journals	Monographs Speeches Reports Studies Newspapers Contracts Hearings Minutes Plans	Monographs Speeches Reports Studies Newspapers Contracts Hearings Minutes Plans	Speeches Newspapers Hearings Minutes Newspapers	Campaigns Proposals Books Speeches Reports Budgets Journals	Speeches Newspapers Hearings Minutes Manuscripts
University of Maine System	By Inference: Policy Behavior		Policy Behavior	Means of Intervention	Policy Behavior	Participation Means of Intervention	Participation Means of Intervention	Means of Intervention	Means of Intervention
Land Grant Campus	Policy		Policy	Opinion Beliefs	Opinion Beliefs	Opinion Beliefs	Opinion Beliefs	Opinion Beliefs	Opinion
Other Campuses	Policy		Policy	Statements of Opinion	Statements of Opinion	Statements of Opinion	Statements of Opinion	Statements of Opinion	Statements of Opinion

Table 3.1: Kinds of Data Collected and Inferences Drawn (see Yin, 1994, p. 43)

3: Research Problem and Method

Major Reports, University of Maine System

Date	State of Maine Reports Examined During This Study	Synopsis
1966	The First Business of Our Times: A Report to the Advisory Commission for the Higher Education Study	The Academy for Educational Development's formative consulting report establishing the mechanical and philosophical basis behind university restructuring
1966	Report of the Advisory Commission for the Higher Education Study	Helped to reshape the University of Maine System into a unified governance structure
1970	Higher Education in Maine: Its Facilities and Utilization	A facilities planning document prepared by the nationally known Institute for Educational Development
1972	Higher Education Planning for Maine	A thorough planning document providing philosophical guidance for the new system as it attempts to carry out the mandates of the Advisory Commission
1972	Higher Education Facilities Planning Grant: University of Maine at Portland-Gorham	An early and insightful attempt to advocate for access for lifelong learners
1984	Education: Maine's Most Important Investment	An advocacy-based report serving as the impetus for the creation of the Visiting Committee
1985	The University and the Future	An accumulation of ten task force subcommittee reports evaluating System capabilities
1986	Report of the Visiting Committee to the University of Maine	The single-most important study of the System, this document's recommendations served as a master plan in many ways, redirecting trustee priorities and bolstering legislative resolve

-Continued on next page-

3: Research Problem and Method

Date	State of Maine Reports Examined During This Study	Synopsis
1987	Internal Review and Assessment of Development Capabilities and External Planning Study for $25,000,000 Capital Campaign	Ketchum, Inc., contracted with the System to study fund-raising capacity and evaluate perceptions of the System
1990	Report of the Commission to Assess the Impact of Increased State Spending on the University of Maine System	A government accountability report interrupted by a severe decline in the economy and university expropriation
1992	Positioning the University of Maine for the 21st Century: Project 2002	A basic outline of Trustee initiatives over a ten-year period.
1996	The University of Maine System: A Time for Change	An independent assessment of the University System advocating change to a decentralized governance structure
1996	Report of the Commission on Higher Education Governance	The most comprehensive government-conducted report of Maine higher education since the Visiting Committee
1997	Higher Education in Maine: The University of Maine, Science and Engineering, and Maine's Future	A report by George Jacobson and the "Faculty Five" outlining the importance of science and engineering
1997	The Strategic Environmental Assessment of the University of Maine System	A comprehensive best practices study and evaluation of the University of Maine System conducted by the Margaret Chase Smith Center for Public Policy and presented to the Trustees and Chancellor
1998	Higher Education Achievement in Maine	A Maine Development Foundation Report advocating lower tuition and better community college access
1998	Final Report of the Joint Select Committee on Research and Development	Various recommendations for the state to invest in various infrastructure and research and development projects
1999	The Establishment of Ph.D. Programs within the University of Maine System	A recommendation by the Chancellor to a legislative panel to create Ph.D. programs in computer science, molecular genetics, and electrical engineering

Table 3.2: Major Reports, University of Maine System

Threats to Validity

Proper analysis of the data listed in Table 3.1 was critical in the execution of this model. Yin believes that the most important advantage presented by using multiple sources of evidence "is the development of converging lines of inquiry" (Yin, 1994, p. 93). The problem of construct validity is therefore addressed using multiple sources of evidence to provide multiple measures and descriptions of the same phenomenon (Yin, p. 92). This is consistent with the goals and methods of content analysis. Using this methodology, this case study combined a cross-section approach with time-series analysis without some of the implications that result from other complex approaches, such as data paneling.

Nevertheless, discrepancies between descriptions existed in the data to a minor degree. In order to mitigate this variable, this research provides lengthy contextual material as a part of the historical component. You will notice this in the work presented in Chapter 4.

Finally, it must be noted that the author of this work has served in both the Maine House of Representatives and the Maine Senate for a total of eight years, and has served as an assistant professor at a private college in Maine for eight years previous to the legislative service. Being involved in higher education in Maine for over half of the University of Maine's history brings viewpoints. The model of data analysis is designed to mitigate this problem.

CHAPTER FOUR: GROWTH AND DEVELOPMENT OF THE UNIVERSITY OF MAINE SYSTEM

> *Few state constitutions in this country were written, or have been rewritten or amended, to recognize either the importance of or the public's responsibility for providing higher education. Most state constitutions acknowledge the public responsibility for elementary and secondary education; some comment on the education of teachers. But public policy regarding higher education in most states has emerged from actions of the colleges and universities themselves, legislatures, and governors.*
>
> From: *The First Business of Our Times: A Report to the Advisory Commission for the Higher Education Study* (State of Maine, 1966, September 30, p. 14)

Introduction to the Political History

Starting in this chapter we will chronologically explore the events and decisions of chancellors, governors, legislators, and the various trustees who have served the State of Maine since the University of Maine System's inception in 1968 (see Table 4.1). There was a necessity to orient the chapter by governor and chancellor, especially because the rotational appointment configuration of the Board of Trustees of the University of Maine System rendered individual board identification fruitless. Nevertheless, within the next several pages and in the concluding analysis, the contemplations, decisions, and actions of the Board are documented based on several sources of information, including minutes, reports, newspaper articles, budgets, and the comments of individual trustees.

One phenomenon occurring during the System's history was the near-parallel alignment of the terms of chancellors and governors. Consider the terms of office:

4: Growth and Development of the System

Terms of Office of Governors and Chancellors Since 1968

Governors	Year	Chancellors
Curtis	1969	McNeil
Curtis	1970	McNeil
Curtis	1971	McNeil
Curtis	1972	McNeil
Curtis	1973	McNeil
Curtis	1974	McNeil
Longley	1975	**Stanley Freeman/McCarthy
Longley	1976	McCarthy
Longley	1977	McCarthy
Longley	1978	McCarthy
Brennan	1979	McCarthy
Brennan	1980	McCarthy
Brennan	1981	McCarthy
Brennan	1982	McCarthy
Brennan	1983	McCarthy
Brennan	1984	McCarthy
Brennan	1985	McCarthy
Brennan	1986	McCarthy/*JackFreeman/ Woodbury
McKernan	1987	Woodbury
McKernan	1988	Woodbury
McKernan	1989	Woodbury
McKernan	1990	Woodbury
McKernan	1991	Woodbury
McKernan	1992	Woodbury
McKernan	1993	Woodbury
McKernan	1994	Orenduff
King	1995	Orenduff
King	1996	Orenduff/**Woodbury
King	1997	MacTaggart
King	1998	MacTaggart
King	1999	MacTaggart

* Jack Freeman served as chancellor for a two-week period, leaving in July
**Major Interim

Table 4.1 Chancellors of the University of Maine System

4: *Growth and Development of the System* 47

Evidence from this study indicated that factors external to the University of Maine System caused the alignment phenomenon to occur, rather than traditional or typical means of replacement of a chancellor by a governing board. As you will read over the course of the next hundred pages, one chancellor was effectively forced out by a governor, one by a legislator, and one by the System's faculty.

What follows from this point until the conclusion of Chapter 4 is, in effect, the history and politics of the University of Maine System. The sections are subcategorized by three distinct phases of University System history. As will be seen, legislators, administrators, trustees, the media, students, and others are identified according to a loose chronological sequencing within a subheading identified by either a governor's reign or a chancellor's administration. While many of the events that occurred in these periods were due in part to their leadership, a great deal of information in each subsection simply documents major events that took place during each era.

The First Phase: The Early Years (1968-1974)
The early years of the University of Maine System were guided by two individuals and were buttressed by commission work and studies. The two men that helped to guide the new organization were Governor Kenneth M. Curtis and Chancellor Donald R. McNeil. The first four studies listed previously in Table 3.2 (and to a lesser extent the fifth) were documents that these men were very familiar with. These were the basis from which major decisions about the University of Maine System were made.

The Administration of Governor Kenneth M. Curtis (1967-1974)
Governor Ken Curtis served as chief executive of the State of Maine from 1967 through 1974. These would turn out to be the formative years for the University of Maine System under its current governance structure.

Governor Curtis took office at the young age of thirty-five as a registered Democrat from Manchester, Maine. Curtis was a popular and respected Maine citizen before, during, and after his stint in office. The literature made it appear quite possible that one of the reasons for his long-term popularity was his constant devotion to Maine's system of higher education. Although not the true architect of the new state university system, Curtis was perfectly timed and philosophically well equipped to be the guiding hand for its formation and modernization.

The One Hundred and Second Legislature and Governor Reed set the stage for the success of a unified University of Maine System. Reed was a Republican who served two terms prior to the election of Governor Curtis, and during his tenure the State had initiated an examination of the way in which public higher education was offered to Maine citizens. Reed coined the phrase "the first business of our times," and he made the issue of higher education a centerpiece of his administration (State of Maine, 1966, Letter of Transmittal). The Advisory Commission for the Higher Education Study (also known as the Coles Commission) had already been established when Governor Curtis was sent to the capital, and several reports were at his disposal.

One major report that was drafted by a panel of consultants was entitled "The First Business of Our Times' (State of Maine, 1966). The report closely mirrored the vision for higher education that Governor Curtis held. A University of Maine System established and governed for all campuses under one board was recommended. With this vision came the hope for several major advantages over the prior system of fragmented, independent, state-controlled campuses of the early 1960s. The new system's potential strengths were outlined in "The First Business of Our Times" report (State of Maine, 1966). According to the report, in this type of system:

a. unnecessary duplication of certain education programs is avoided;
b. appropriate duplication of other education programs is assured;
c. the broadest variety of education programs possible is made available in or close to centers of population;
d. the proliferation of uneconomical specialized institutions, services, or facilities is avoided; and
e. the transferability of credits within the system is maximized (State of Maine, 1966, p. 32).

In a unified, statewide University of Maine System, it was thought that there would be "unusual opportunities to eliminate program and facility duplications and to greatly strengthen program offerings throughout the state" (State of Maine, 1966, p. 32).

4: Growth and Development of the System

Governor Curtis quickly went to work, planning for the passage of a new system. In a speech to The One Hundred and Third Legislature, Governor Curtis sought assurances for its establishment:

> Education is truly the "first order of business of our times." Because of the recommendations presented by the Advisory Commission for Higher Education Study, higher education is certainly the first order of business of this One Hundred and Third Legislature. The Advisory Commission includes some of Maine's most distinguished and knowledgeable citizens. You and I have the responsibility of giving immediate consideration to all facets of their study and recommendations. The State of Maine clearly deserves and must have a better system of higher education. I expect this report and your action will provide the catalyst necessary to determine our goals and means. (Curtis, 1967, January 26, p. 7)

Curtis believed strongly that a centralized system governed by a chancellor and board of trustees was the proper governance structure needed at that time to assure equity and opportunity and to reduce unnecessary overlap and duplication of programs. He had another important goal in mind, however, that was less apparent to the legislature until later years. Curtis saw the potential for an equally successful building and construction program for higher education. His "Budget Message Address" of January 9, 1969, pushed forward ambitious building goals, as he related in the following excerpt from the speech:

> I have divided this program into six bond issues, each dealing with a special area of State responsibility. For the University of Maine, which now includes the State Colleges, I propose a capital improvement program of $22,855,000. This program was prepared by the Board of Trustees of the University according to their biennial priorities. It provides for major improvements throughout the University system. (Curtis, 1969, January 9, p. 3)

Curtis went on to detail specific components of the plan and the benefits to each campus. Unfortunately for the Governor, these goals

4: Growth and Development of the System

were too ambitious and the bond issue was defeated by Maine citizens in that fall's referendum.

In another 1969 address to the Legislature, the Governor continued to stress the role and importance of higher education. His "Special Message on Education" again prioritized higher education. His support was unwavering and, while giving the Legislature credit for adopting overarching policies, facilities plans, and consolidation, he now requested that legislative leaders turn their attention to growth:

> During the next two years, the University of Maine expects to open its doors to an additional seventeen hundred students. This increase alone will require substantial new appropriations, but simply setting more students as our goal is insufficient. We must do our best to improve the breadth and quality of the education offered. To do so means salaries for staff at a level competitive with other institutions, and equipment, facilities, and libraries compatible with the needs of education in this complicated age. (Curtis, 1969, February 11, p. 6)

Curtis also supported a wide variety of changes in educational law designed to improve the managerial capabilities of the chancellor's office and the Board of Trustees. In addition, he recommended sizable supplemental appropriations during off-biennial budget years, such as the $6.525 million boost in 1971 for "an additional 1,200 students, for cost-of-living salary increases, and for urgently needed support of one- and two-year educational programs" (Curtis, 1971, January 13, p. 4).

In Fort Kent, Maine, on September 28, 1970, the minutes of the Board of Trustees clearly show a developing relationship with the Governor's office. Although there would be many peaks and valleys to the relationship between the Trustees and sitting governors, it was clear from the beginning that Governor Curtis, the System's first governor, was interested in being involved with the University System's growth and development. Governor Curtis had good communications with the Trustees, as shown by the following entry in the Board of Trustee's minutes: "Potential legislation: The Governor has asked to have a brief of any legislation that the University might want to submit to the 105th Legislature, by October 15, 1970" (Board of Trustees of the University of Maine System, 1970, September 28, p. 10).

4: Growth and Development of the System

As a result of this developing relationship, the board voted to develop several legislative requests with respect to issues, including the exercise of eminent domain by the University System, which had become clouded due to a recent court ruling. Other requests included plans relating to community college development, the evolution of a state scholarship, an American Indian education bill, educational television, and others.

As Curtis prepared to leave office, most University of Maine System supporters looked at the Governor's years in office with fondness, particularly because of his active role. He established a helpful but hands-off relationship. The role of the University System was now clearly defined in statute through the work of the Higher Education Planning Commission that was established and began its work in 1969. "The First Operational Report from the Higher Education Planning Commission" was the most detailed report on higher education that Maine had seen. In Chapter 14 of that report, university governance was described, and further refinements specifically aimed at the roles of the board, faculty, and method of tenure systems were recommended. A passage from the proposal set the stage for governance roles and responsibilities:

> At the core of governance is the establishment, recognition, and acceptance of authority and responsibilities, including respect for people and the protection of their rights. Also fundamental is the principle that the creation of the structure of governance shall be in conformity with the foundational concept that all groups within the University--trustees, administrators, faculty, alumni, and students; and various communities outside the University--are intricately and delicately interrelated in the total effort of the University as an institution of education. (Higher Education Planning Commission, 1972, p. 99)

With the intended establishment of tenure, higher faculty wages, and more faculty responsibility in university governance that resulted from this document, interests from all sides of the University of Maine System heaped praise on the Governor. Governor Curtis was proud of what he and others had built. Many years later, in 1996, he would admit that not all of the goals of the System were met with success. He would again suggest bold reform rather than incremental approaches as the solution to the problems that the University of Maine System faced in the late 1990s.

The Term of Chancellor Donald R. McNeil (1969-1974)

Were it not for major policy development in the State of Maine that involved the consolidation of all state-held university resources, there would have been no record in Maine of Donald R. McNeil. It was the final 1968 compromise state legislation that led to a unified University of Maine System that drew the interest of McNeil, a rising administrator in the Wisconsin public higher education system.

During the late 1960s and early 1970s, the new unified system in Maine was widely known as "The Super U" (Hertz, 1972, January 31, p. 1). Despite the fact that the Maine Legislature and Governor Curtis were able to achieve their vision for a new and restructured University of Maine System, the years were characterized by growing pains and uncertainty. For example, the first two bond issues that Maine voters faced following the restructuring were defeated by a clear majority of voters, one in November 1969 and the other in June 1970. No bond issues were successful during the first three and a half years of Chancellor McNeil's term. In a *Bangor Daily News* article analyzing the reasons for the bond-proposal defeats, the sheer size of the new Super U was cited as a major factor behind voter uneasiness:

> Bigness and the spending of bigness worry the average taxpayer the most. While acknowledging that inflation and tight money force costs up, a majority of people contacted in an informal poll felt that too much money was being spent by the university. Or worse, they didn't know what that money was doing or where it was going. (Hertz, 1972, January 31, p. 1)

New system goals such as avoiding unnecessary duplication, improving student transferability of credits, and centralizing common university services remained only partially achieved through the McNeil years while university spending and tuition costs rose dramatically. But the growing pains beleaguering the University of Maine System in its

4: Growth and Development of the System

infancy appeared to root within the public's perception of not only how large the structure was, but how the System was managed.

Chancellor McNeil himself may have inadvertently turned the public against the Super U upon his arrival, and an abundance of criticism seemed to follow his every move. A native of Spokane, Washington, with a Ph.D. in history from the University of Wisconsin, McNeil was a chancellor for the University Extension of Wisconsin before being hired as Maine's first chancellor on March 1, 1969 (Hertz, 1972, February 2, p. 1). Part of the agreement made upon hiring McNeil was that he would be able to choose the location for the Office of Chancellor. Rather than establishing his headquarters near the land-grant institution in Orono or at the state capitol in Augusta, McNeil unexpectedly chose instead to locate his office in Portland, across from the University of Southern Maine. This initial decision drew criticism not only by those in education circles, but Maine voters and taxpayers soon displayed their wrath based on this and other decisions, and their displeasure continued throughout his six-year tenure.

McNeil chose a home in the luxurious seashore community of Cape Elizabeth that was paid for as part of a fringe-benefit package; but when "flak" developed, the University System Board of Trustees backed off and made arrangements for an annual $5,000 home-payment allowance instead (Hertz, 1972, February 2, p. 3). Several reports claimed that he was Maine's highest paid state official, and other job benefits such as employing a chauffeur simply did not sit well with some Maine citizens. Unfortunately, other conflicts flared periodically during the six years, and these were buoyed by swiftly rising tuition costs, escalating from $100 to $450 at the state colleges and from $350 to $550 at the Orono campus by the end of McNeil's tenure (Harkavy, 1974, February 9, p. 22). Some observers were quick to point out that high tuition costs were keeping low-income Mainers from attending college.

As if cost wasn't enough of a concern, the faculty at several campuses raised the issue of quality in 1971 and 1972, claiming that they were "powerless and far removed from the power center" (Hertz, 1972, February 2, p. 1). The basis for faculty unrest centered on their inability to authorize new programs, a power that they once held under the old system and a problem that compounded due to the belief that they could not "rub shoulders with the chancellor" (Hertz, p. 1). Administrators agreed with faculty, complaining that critical new programs could not be

4: Growth and Development of the System

implemented without going through McNeil, and they lamented that the legislature had "created something antithetical to Maine people" (Hertz, p. 1). At one point, faculty threatened to boycott the graduate program if binding arbitration was not accepted as a dispute-resolution mechanism for disagreements about program offerings. Although dissenters were also noted on the University of Maine Board of Trustees, the Board did give McNeil an official (but close) vote of confidence in 1971, angering some faculty. This was likely the first of many occurrences during the history of the System in which the Board of Trustees was considered by some to be disconnected with the wishes of the general public, the faculty, and some administrators.

At the Orono campus, the Student Senate called for McNeil's resignation following a 1972 budget revelation that pegged the cost of operating the chancellor's office at $280,000, most of which "could better be used for education," according to one student dissident (Hansen, 1972, January 21, p. 30). The lion's share of that cost went into salaries, and the size and cost of the central administration became a favorite target of critics, despite repeated efforts to explain savings recouped through the centralization of services.

The student rebellion was mild compared to the bombshell leveled by gubernatorial candidate James Longley in September 1974. Longley stated that if elected, he would find a replacement for McNeil and appoint a citizens' committee to restructure the board (Steele, 1974, November 7, p. 21). Longley was generally viewed by Mainers as a deficit hawk who, if elected, would quickly go to work to reduce spending in areas that he felt were mismanaged or included wasteful spending; the University of Maine System was included in both of those categories by the candidate.

Longley was in an excellent position to be critical of the System. He had chaired the so-called Longley Commission in 1972-1973, which was "originated by a resolve of the Republican legislature, was structured by a Democratic governor, and was financed and conducted by the Maine business community," according to Winthrop C. Libby, President of the University of Maine campus at Orono (Libby, October 3, 1973, p. 18). Major proposals from the Longley Commission, such as merging the vocational technical colleges with the University of Maine System to form a single administration, were virtually ignored by the educational community and the System. Longley traced the resistance to a structure

4: Growth and Development of the System

that was beginning to understand the power of its built-in autonomy to outside influences. In addition, Longley bitterly complained during the campaign that the University of Maine System had lobbied unethically against his campaign. Longley gauged voter dissension against the Super U and was publicly critical; as a result, he was viewed unfavorably by some administrators in Maine's higher education community.

If the election of James Longley as Maine's Governor in 1974 was one of the biggest political surprises in Maine history, the resignation of Chancellor McNeil was one of the smallest. Despite the Chancellor's insistence that he had no intention of leaving the University of Maine System, it took only one month after Longley's election for McNeil to announce his resignation and take a post as an executive director of California's first Post Secondary Education Commission. Governor-elect Longley made it clear that he did not want McNeil serving in the chancellor's office during his term, and speculation from editorial staffs grew that Longley might somehow find a way to fire him. According to law, it appeared that a Maine governor did not have the authority to do this. Fortunately, before Governor Longley was sworn into office, McNeil took the hint and found a new job in another state.

With so many growing pains stretched out over one administration, what can be said about the leadership exhibited by Donald McNeil? There are few positives outlined in the literature. In the first several years of the new University of Maine System, there was an expectation that the road would be rocky, so many of those difficult times were anticipated. One accomplishment that was credited to his administration was the successful completion of the accreditation process for all campuses. When Chancellor McNeil came to work for the University of Maine in 1969, there were still three campuses (i.e., Presque Isle, Fort Kent, and Machias) that were not accredited at all. Although some legislators believed that the campuses were on their way to accreditation, the Chancellor apparently felt that the unified university structure gave visiting committees and accreditation boards the faith they needed to finally make their decisions.

A second hallmark of the McNeil years was the steady growth of the student population at each of the campuses. With increases in the student population came some increases in the number of classes and programs offered. In addition, McNeil presided over the name changes of each university campus (Board of Trustees of the University of Maine System, 1970, April 10, p. 1).

Chancellor McNeil had hoped to guide the University of Maine System into the field of medicine as well. He hired a special consultant in 1972 in an attempt to offer a school of medicine without the expense of major construction. At the time of his resignation, the concept was little more than a proposal that had struggled through two years of tortuous debate, spilling into the gubernatorial elections of 1974. The proposal became a lightning rod for those who thought that university spending was out of control. These dissenters were joined by a faculty-splitting debate over whether the System was spending enough time, energy, and resources to assure quality within current programs and related new programs. As will be seen, Governor Longley's opposition to the proposal made likelihood of its realization very low.

The Second Phase: 1975-1986

The second phase of the University of Maine System (as defined here) includes the terms of Governor James B. Longley and Governor Joseph E. Brennan. During these years, Patrick E. McCarthy occupied the chancellor's office with one very brief exception, Chancellor Jack E. Freeman, who lasted just two weeks in office. In addition, this section details Acting Chancellor, Stanley L. Freeman, because his term as an interim was marked by several important events.

The Term of Acting Chancellor Stanley L. Freeman (12/1974 to 8/1975)

Under normal circumstances, interested parties might not spend a lot of time thinking about the accomplishments of an interim chancellor. The resignation of Don McNeil, coupled with the political environment under new Governor James Longley, led to circumstances that were far from normal, however, and the demands on the Acting Chancellor were great.

Stanley Freeman was a graduate of Maine's Bates College and later attended Columbia University Teachers College (Beeny, 1974, December 10). He inherited a mandate to reestablish a relationship with a governor who had forced out his predecessor and demanded the

4: Growth and Development of the System

resignation of trustees. The belief that prevailed among those in higher education appeared to reflect outright hostility between university administrators and Governor Longley. Freeman's first priority in the hostile environment was reflected in one of his first official statements. Acting Chancellor Freeman pledged to do the following:

> ...establish effective working relationships with the Governor's Office and members of the legislature so that the University's capacity to meet the needs of Maine citizens during the next two years is adequately sustained by both dollar appropriations and a well-placed belief in the educative process. (Beeny, 1974, December 10, p. 1)

Freeman had served as staff director for the higher education planning commission during the transition of the fragmented campuses into one system, so he had a strong knowledge of the growth and development of the system. Unfortunately for Freeman, he had also directly supervised the planning effort for the medical school proposal, so the Longley Administration was guarded in its approach to the Acting Chancellor.

From 1969 to 1974, legislative appropriations to the University of Maine System had doubled, rising from 17.2 to 36.4 million dollars (Beeny, 1974, December 10, p. 1). Without the hope to maintain funding at current levels, the administration had little choice but to look in a different direction. During the hard economic times of the early and mid-1970s, the people of Maine were clearly in the mood for belt-tightening. It was the responsibility of Freeman to present cuts to the Governor and the Legislature during the first few months of 1975, rather than to wait for the next chancellor to be appointed.

The mood of Mainers toward the System was harsh in 1974. The battleground became the University of Maine System's agency structure, which featured an independence from legislative intervention. The battle lines were drawn. The legislative guardian of the University of Maine System quickly became the Chairman of the Joint Standing Committee on Education, State Senator Bennett D. Katz of Augusta. Katz spearheaded a committee report released in March 1975 that emphasized the importance of the University of Maine System's independence from legislative interference. According to the report, the legislature should

58   4: Growth and Development of the System

carry out its responsibilities "without becoming involved in the internal affairs of the University" and, in addition, "the legislature has consistently refused to meddle in the internal affairs" of the System (Vanderweide, March 20, 1975, p. 33).

Despite legislative interventions, the Governor attempted to make good on his promise to request the resignation of the members of the Board of Trustees of the University of Maine System. Members of the Board of Trustees, including chairperson Jean Sampson, ignored the Governor's request, but Longley's resignation demand ran deeper than a mere shot over the bow. To Longley, the University of Maine System had overstepped its bounds by heavily lobbying the legislature with new program requests. Governor Longley claimed that the System had shamelessly lobbied the legislature and spent as much as $500,000 "promoting a medical school at a time when there are serious questions in the minds of most citizens of this state whether a medical school is feasible and can be afforded at this time" (Day, 1975, February 15, p. 1). The effect of Longley's claim may have resonated with the public more by reason of the economy and the previous administration's spending priorities than by the two full years of university lobbying that took place.

With controversy swirling around the board, the chancellorship, and the structure of the agency, the new Acting Chancellor was forced to present a budget full of deep cuts and restructuring. Chancellor Freeman established an "austerity program designed to save the University of Maine about $70,000," concentrating on hiring, overtime pay, travel, and communication expenses ("U. of M. Takes Steps," 1975, February 14, p. 36). The program turned out to be only the beginning of the massive cuts required by the failing economy and a Governor determined to get spending in line.

The height of the challenge presented to Freeman came midway through his six-month stint as Acting Chancellor. His proposed budget included an $848,715 cut that eliminated some academic minors; a $416,980 reduction in research and public service funding; a $960,208 cut in administrative services; a $280,000 reduction in personnel and student services; and the threat that the System could not guarantee some students that they could finish in the programs they had started ("High Stakes Poker," 1975, March 8, p. 4). An editorial column in the *Kennebec Journal* offered the following synopsis:

4: Growth and Development of the System

What Freeman did not say is that the University's previously loose-reined budget is the product of a system that fosters irresponsible overspending. Academic freedom is a goal to be fervently sought, but academic license isn't the same thing and that's what it amounts to with a budget in which the specifics are buried or not even known. Governor Longley made it his job to know... ("High Stakes Poker," 1975, March 8, p. 4).

Apparently Freeman, a professor by trade, felt pressure from having to offer such deep and divisive cuts in his new role. Following Freeman's presentation of the System's budget to the Legislature, Longley accused Freeman of hinting that the Governor wished to close one of the University System campuses (Day, 1975, March 8, p. 13). Longley quickly raised the issue and claimed foul, calling the statement nothing more than a scare tactic; Freeman accepted the explanation of the Governor (Day, p. 13). Governor Longley railed at Freeman and the Board of Trustees:

> Once again I plead with the University trustees to recognize the needs of this state and the already overburdened taxpayers and the elderly and low income who I feel have as great a priority of relief than the need for the University for more millions to spend as it sees fit. ("Longley Again Defends Budget", 1975, March 29, p. 26)

The Trustees may or may not have been ready for the about-face that they were to soon experience.

Whether historians should consider the political climate for the University of Maine System under Governor Longley harsh cannot be properly evaluated without an examination of the failed medical school proposal. Over three years after Chancellor McNeil had appointed a special assistant to develop a medical school without walls, the idea finally died under the Governor's hand. The Board of Trustees endorsed an original concept in 1972 to develop a school for training doctors that would utilize existing buildings and the facilities of some major hospitals in order to avoid major capital outlays ("Dr. Oliver Cope Named," 1972, March 16, p. 14). The concept faced tough sledding, especially given the severe economic climate, the failed higher education bond issues, the Governor's resignation requests, and the perceived free-spending reputation that the University of Maine System developed under Chancellor McNeil.

The medical school was to be governed under the University of Maine System umbrella, according to a bill proposed in the Maine Legislature early in 1975. To make matters worse for supporters of the medical school concept, Governor Longley again took aim at the Trustees during the legislative debate, this time claiming that the University System had spent thousands of dollars lobbying the Maine Legislature with taxpayer money. "I feel strongly that to use taxpayer money in this fashion...is a fraud on the taxpayers of this state," wrote the Governor in a harshly worded letter to the board chair (Steele, 1975, May 21, p. 1). Longley instructed the Board to "immediately correct this abuse in fairness to hardworking, dedicated legislators and in the interest of economical and efficient government." He questioned the project's estimated cost as possibly being ten times below potential actual costs, keeping Acting Chancellor Freeman and the Trustees on the defensive (Steele, p. 1).

In the end, Freeman could do little more than watch as Rome burned. Governor Longley's veto of the medical school may have had a more profound effect on the future of the University of Maine System than any other action of the executive branch, the legislative branch, or the agency itself, and it was highly ironic that it had to happen under Freeman's watch. The full text of the Governor's veto message is in Appendix A.

The Administration of Governor James B. Longley (1975-1978)

Governor James B. Longley will be remembered by many in Maine as a man of great political will. In his race for office, many polls had the independent in last place in a three-way race only a few weeks before Election Day. His victory stunned onlookers from around the country and energized critics of the two-party system.

Governor Longley was a champion to the fiscal conservatives. During his tenure, he was a proponent of keeping taxes in check and practicing good fiscal responsibility. Governor Longley was, to the opponents of big-government and big spending, just what the State of Maine needed to deal with the complicated times of the 1970s. As a self-proclaimed independent, he served as governor without the luxury of

4: Growth and Development of the System 61

being able to rely on a block of legislators to help him forward his agenda.

Was Governor Longley's anti-public higher education reputation justified? To fully consider this question, an examination of Jim Longley's earlier years, both in and out of office, needs to be assessed.

Jim Longley made a huge splash into the debate over the future of higher education in 1973 when he chaired an independent committee charged with looking at public financial practices in Maine. The committee, composed mostly of Maine businesspeople, was highly critical of the University of Maine System's operations; as a result, they offered sixty-five recommendations to the state on how the University could run more efficiently (Reilly, 1978, April 13, p. 1). The group was known as the Maine Management and Cost Survey, and their work served as a springboard for Longley's candidacy for the Office of Governor of the State of Maine. Because most of the controversial cost-saving recommendations were ignored, Longley's criticism of university leadership grew. Nevertheless, he and others who had views on the fast growth of public spending were ignored. "The chancellor pretty much said get lost," according to trustee Robert Masterson, a Portland banker (Reilly, p. 1).

Candidate Longley steadfastly clung to his belief that the University System needed to be accountable for high spending levels. His surprise victory came as a shock to System officials, whom he had accused during the campaign of lobbying hard against his election. Longley's early years in office were characterized by serious battles with chancellors, trustees, and other administrators. These battles included the resignation of Chancellor McNeil, who Longley probably would have tried to fire; a request for the resignation of the entire board of trustees; substantive cuts in the university budgets, including an austerity program; and the death of a university proposal to create a medical school without walls.

Governor Longley's impact on the system of higher education in Maine is difficult to assess. The literature at the time expressed both fears and cheers for his commitment to holding the line on spending. An historical analysis on the impact of the Longley years on Maine higher education probably should not be documented without noting the tremendous level of financial support from his predecessor. There was also the lingering perception in Maine that the budgets of Chancellor

4: Growth and Development of the System

McNeil were left unchecked. It has already been pointed out in this analysis that under Governor Curtis, the University of Maine System was brought into being and handsomely supported with dollars never before seen. In Governor Longley's view and the view of many rank and file legislators, these cash-drained years were a good time to level off spending increases and allow the System to catch up with itself. This leveling off did not occur without opposition from an indignant Board of Trustees.

According to a *Portland Press Herald* story in 1976, Governor Longley's stance in his early years in office was characterized as "adamantly against finding more funds for UMaine" (Rosenfeld, 1976, April 1, p. 1). The article said that the Governor was "not convinced school trustees have done everything in their power to make ends meet" (Rosenfeld, p. 1). During those all-too-recent times of high interest rates, high inflation, and energy shortages that plagued the early 1970s, Governor Longley's position had been understandable to most, but disheartening to some. The 1976 *Portland Press Herald* column was not about Longley's steadfast position. Rather, the headline read, "Longley Relaxes Stance on Aid for University" (Rosenfeld, p. 1). As the economy began to turn for the better, so did Longley's support for the System. According to the article, "Longley said he could support 'reasonable' spending for the university if it did not require additional taxes and did not upset other priority projects" (Rosenfeld, p. 1). Small spending increases did ensue.

Longley believed that in the long run there was no problem in Maine "that more jobs won't help" (Larrabee, 1976, p. 25). His focus on better jobs through stimulation of the competitive marketplace in Maine spilled over into the educational debate in 1975 and continued through 1976 and 1977. One Longley proposal for secondary schools, for example, sought to place all funds collected by towns through local property taxes into the State's general fund. Using this approach, "the needs of education could be examined on a priority basis with the needs of other areas and appropriations could be made accordingly," Longley explained (Associated Press, 1975, p. 1). University experts in secondary education were thought to be very critical of the plan. Longley lashed out at some, stating, "I fully realize that there have been some in the university community and elsewhere who have tried to paint me as being anti-education....Somewhere along the line, some educators seemed to get the

4: Growth and Development of the System

impression that they were free to challenge everyone else, but that they were not supposed to be challenged from the outside" (Associated Press, p. 1).

Some in the educational establishment did not take kindly to another proposal formed on the basis of competitive environments. In Governor Longley's 1977 "Budget Message Address," a voucher plan was proposed for students entering higher education in Maine:

> The education budget we are presenting, we feel, will provide more direct assistance to what must become our real 'bottom line' in education...*the student.* We will ask for your approval of a $1.5 million voucher plan, which will enable deserving students throughout the State to receive state grants to attend any post-secondary school of their choice in Maine. (Longley, 1977, p. 4)

Many in the educational establishment feared the arrival of a funding plan entirely based on vouchers. A review of Longley's statements during this period revealed that their fears were thoroughly justified. Defeat of this proposal came swiftly.

Although Longley may not have left a legacy that some in the educational establishment care to recall, some Maine citizens remember him as a strong decision-maker. Longley did not believe that more money was the answer to every problem, and he stuck to his beliefs throughout his tenure as Governor.

Keeping promises with Maine citizens was a high priority to Governor Longley; ultimately, he kept his promise to Maine citizens by not running for reelection in 1978.

A *Bangor Daily News* headline following the one and only term of Governor James Longley summed up his impact on the system rather succinctly: "Longley's Effect on Super-U to Outlive Term" (Reilly, 1978, April 13, p. 1). The areas of Longley's impression were broad and represented the supreme use of all of the tools available to a governor within in a unified system of university governance. In the case of Longley, the changes that were imposed on the System were the result of a great deal of political infighting, disagreement over university policy, and the Governor's steadfast support of fiscal responsibility over unchecked or irresponsible growth.

A review of the impact of Longley's decisions would have to begin with an analysis of the medical-school resolution. One could argue that the decisions made in the mid-1970s have had a colossal significance in Maine even today, not just to the system of higher education but to the economy as well. Consider, for example, the case of the University of New England located in Biddeford, Maine. In the late 1970s and early 1980s, the University of New England, then called St. Francis College, was on the verge of financial ruin. The profitability of Maine's small private colleges was under great strain from a myriad of economic, programmatic, and demographic shortcomings. In fact, Nasson College, located just a few miles west of St. Francis, did not survive, closing its doors in 1983 following a failed attempt to merge the two colleges. St. Francis and other local colleges received a small boost in upper-class enrollments from the many transferring students leaving Nasson College for the 1983-1984 academic year. Nevertheless, without a new vision of what the University of New England should be, a probability of failure of that campus was real.

It is reasonable to speculate that because there was still no statewide medical school for Maine students, the decision by the University of New England to improve its emphasis on medicine gave the school a giant niche that many believe has led to the recent phenomenal success of this private university. It appears that the medical-school gap, ultimately filled by private enterprise, may serve as an example to states with similar agency structures that are attempting to review and plan for a better partnership between private and public colleges and universities. The case of the now fully emerged and thriving University of New England, located along Biddeford's oceanfront community, is a potentially rich case study for researchers. What happens when a perceived programmatic/curricular expansion is not addressed by a state's university system? Conversely, how does uninhibited program growth affect the strength and vitality of a state's independent colleges and universities when taxpayer-supported expansions potentially undercut already-established academic programs? There are interesting supply/demand-related issues raised under the Longley Administration that remain un-researched in Maine and many other states even today. Over the years, University of Maine System program expansions in areas

4: Growth and Development of the System

from nursing to marine studies to business administration were criticized by private colleges, in much the same manner that Longley's veto of the medical school was criticized by trustees. The difference was in the perspective.

A critical relationship that requires further exploration in light of this discussion is the method of establishment of a proper balance of programs between the public and private colleges. Who should examine this balance in the wake of the university autonomy created by a unified system such as Maine's? In some states, governments have created boards to examine these issues and to rectify them for the purposes of planning. States with coordinating boards include small states like Nebraska and Montana and large states like New York, Ohio, and Pennsylvania. In Maine, no such coordinating mechanism exists unless a governor or legislature objects to policy established by the trustees. Although the first example of major policy disagreement appeared during the Longley Administration in regard to the medical-school proposal, other examples have appeared over the years. These included scaling back the Education Network of Maine, which had once been proposed as a campus of its own during the administrations of Governor McKernan and Governor King, and the One Hundred Eighteenth Maine Legislature's rejection of a proposal offering free tuition for in-state students during their first two years of public post-secondary schooling. The latter was proposed by the Speaker of the House and President of the Senate in 1998 and endorsed by Chancellor MacTaggart, but opposed by rank and file legislators and Governor King's Administration.

A concurrent conflict during the Longley years that deserves closer examination was his relationship with chancellors and trustees. It has been noted that upon Longley's election, Chancellor McNeil's resignation was nearly immediate. Governor Longley made it quite clear that if McNeil did not leave, he would be fired or somehow forced out of office. Could the Governor have pulled off this feat under the law? The statutes provide for trustee responsibility in this area. Maine residents and onlookers throughout the country will never know; realistically, however, a reigning chancellor operating under an unwilling Governor is possible, legal, but highly unlikely. From that perspective, McNeil's resignation relieved the potential firestorm of political pressure that would have been placed at the feet of the trustees.

Speculation over potential trustee handling of the McNeil affair is further complicated by decisions made by those trustees after his resignation. Trustees refused Longley's demand that they resign from their posts in unison. This prompted a press conference and two biting statements from the Governor. The statement, "I think that the present members of the Board of Trustees should listen to the people of Maine, even if they don't want to listen to the Governor" (Day, 1975, February 15, p. 1), was followed by this terse assessment:

> Of all the departments and agencies of state government, the University was the one most interested in protecting its own interests and the one least interested in the needs of the state as a whole. (Day, 1975, February 15, p. 1)

The appointment of Interim Chancellor Stanley Freeman, the architect of the medical-school proposal, also potentially reflected the belief that trustees had nearly complete autonomy over the System. It can be argued that the Freeman appointment reflected an end-run approval strategy for the medical school that involved going around the Governor and directly through the legislature. The end-run theory is evidenced by several events, including the introduction of a bill into the legislative process, the appointment of Freeman, and the appearance that the "trustees already hired faculty even though the voters of Maine or the legislature have not approved a medical school" (Day, 1975, February 15, p. 1). Whether this end-run was planned or not, the legislature did indeed approve the medical school, forcing a veto by the Governor. Longley's objections to the proposal were detailed, and given their historical significance, the full body of Longley's veto statement is included in Appendix A of this report.

The Term of Chancellor Patrick E. McCarthy (1975-1986)

To students of Maine history, this was one McCarthy of whom even U.S. Senator Margaret Chase Smith approved. The only Maine native among the final two candidates recommended by a trustee search committee, Patrick McCarthy appeared to have no edge going into the final decision of who would be Maine's second full-fledged chancellor.

4: Growth and Development of the System 67

When the other candidate withdrew from contention, however, Maine was left with one of its sons to guide the Super University.

Born in Rumford, Maine, Patrick McCarthy attended elementary school in Bangor and graduated from Bridgton Academy in southwestern Maine before attending college ("Chancellor McCarthy to Quit," 1985, July 23, p. 5). He spent three years as a student at the University of Maine's Orono campus (Steele, 1975, June 5, p. 17).

As was the case with other finalists for the chancellor's post, there were some minor concerns expressed about the candidate. Chancellor McCarthy came equipped with a master's degree in city and regional planning from Harvard University, but had neither a bachelor's nor a doctoral degree (Steele, 1975, June 5, p. 17). From the point of view of some faculty, this was a major shortcoming. According to one department chair, "the naming of McCarthy was quite a disappointment" among academics (Maraghy, 1975, July 6, p. 1). The lack of Ph.D. credentials caused one trustee to vote against the appointment, but the 12-1 vote was described by a major newspaper as "perfectly respectable" ("End of Search," 1975, June 28, p. 24).

Chancellor McCarthy had advanced through the process as a result of his likable personality, to be sure. But it was his ideas and vision that caused twelve trustees to feel comfortable enough to vote for him. McCarthy stressed the need for the University System to strengthen its scholarship, research, and community service (Steele, 1975, June 5, p. 17). In addition, he recognized the current economic situation in Maine and pledged to make each dollar stretch as far as possible (Steele, p. 17). Other major planks included a desire to offer programs that better reflected the needs of the citizens of Maine. His hope was to make the system "so valuable to the people of Maine that they'll be eager to pay a fair share of its costs," which apparently meant that despite stretching dollars, he believed that the System would cost more along the road to improvement (Reilly, 1975, September 4, p. 1). One of those costs would be an increase in faculty salaries. The Chancellor felt strongly that low salaries were having an impact on faculty morale (Reilly, p. 1). His financial support of faculty almost certainly quieted some of the critics of his academic credentials.

The tight economic times offered a great challenge to the incoming Chancellor. In the midst of economic recession in Maine late in 1975, the issue of the day in academia and government was retrenchment. The

4: Growth and Development of the System

University of Maine System would be asked to operate within its means, and give back even more with the passage of a budget package calling for a 10 percent cut ($3.7 million in total) in funding. In response, trustees implemented a one-year freeze on academic enrollments and proposed a $100 per year tuition hike to help fund a $3.5 million pay increase for system employees that had been previously recommended by a panel of Maine businesspeople (Maraghy, 1975, December 4, p. 1). Unfortunately, the proposal required the state to pick up a portion of the increased costs resulting from the pay hike during the teeth of the fiscally conservative Longley years. Given the economic and political climate, a major clash between the University System and government was inevitable.

A special session of the legislature convened early in 1976, and McCarthy hoped to have the 10 percent cut that had been enacted in the year prior to his arrival restored, making the pay raise a reality. He kicked off a $6.4 million fund-raising campaign that sputtered amidst the national retrenchment. During the retrenchment, public confidence in the value of higher education sagged. According to one report, "the economic value of a college diploma in the job market continues to decline, and more and more scholars are pointing out that a person's family background has more to do with his job mobility than his education" (Reilly, 1976, February 4, p. 1).

Although the legislature did offer the University System some relief, economic realities prohibited the plan's realization and the overall percentage cut was set at 7.6 percent (Reilly, 1981, September 30, p. 11). Deep cuts beginning in the 1976-1977 academic year ensued, with dozens of professors released and thousands of dollars cut from department programs ("UMO Newspaper Cites," 1976, October 14, p. 1). What happened following retrenchment represented some tightly coupled events, including the following:

1. Several mixed performance-related articles about the chancellor appeared in press.
2. Legislative proposals were filed to disband the Super-University concept (Reilly, 1976, August 26, p. 1).
3. Legislative proposals were filed to require the University Trustees to report to a legislative oversight committee (Reilly, 1976, August 26, p. 2).

4: Growth and Development of the System

4. The Governor suggested to the trustees on several occasions to require out-of-state students to pay a higher share of their tuition costs rather than being subsidized by the Maine taxpayer.
5. A Trustee subcommittee report was issued on the health and future of the University of Maine System (Irwin, Jr., 1977, January 1, p. 1).
6. Governor Longley released a well-publicized eight-page report criticizing the Chancellor and trustees for another attempt to circumvent his office by going straight to the legislature's appropriations committee for program funding. This report included Longley's promise of not supporting "another dime" of university appropriations beyond his own budget request to the legislature ("McCarthy Insists," 1977, February 8, p. 1).
7. Public criticism by many faculty followed a defeated bond issue for campus building and construction in the fall of 1977. Complaints pitted the lack of major faculty salary increases against a failed bricks-and-mortar approach by administrators (Haimila, 1977, December 16, p. 17).
8. A successful vote occurred to unionize University faculty in the spring of 1978 (Reilly, 1978, May 12, p. 1).

Under the new union, faculty demands escalated to a fevered pitch by the end of 1978. The new bargaining unit went as far as to request that every faculty member have a personal secretary under a clause guaranteeing the "Tools of Their Trade" (Reilly, 1978, November 18, p. 31). Double-digit percentage raises, automatic sabbaticals, and doubling sick-leave days were also requested (Reilly, p. 31). Full medical and dental packages, binding arbitration over disputes, and an inequities fund of $640,000 would be established to assure supplements to women who were not achieving pay equity (Reilly, p. 31).

Under the new administration of Governor Joseph Brennan, faculty began to achieve their goals in 1979 and 1980. During the first two years of his administration, for example, faculty achieved pay raises averaging 10 and 10.5 percent (Reilly, 1981, September 30, p. 11). Brennan had been sympathetic to union concerns during his 1978 campaign; his victory, combined with the new union and an improving economic engine, changed university priorities, faculty and administrative relationships, and even legislative debate. Unfortunately, the sound economy did not last through the early 1980s.

In the waning years of the McCarthy era, the Chancellor was again forced to offer some unpleasant proposals and face other criticisms. Probably the most unacceptable was a proposal to compress the two-semester University System calendar to a period between October 1 and April 1 in order to save $1 million in fuel costs during the energy shortages of the time ("Hot Seat," 1980, April 7, p. 10). A hostile reaction from students and parents prevented this proposal from progressing. Students also criticized the System for its inability to allow for the transfer of credits, which has been an often-repeated complaint throughout the System's entire life span (Reilly, 1981, March 17, p. 1). Further criticism by faculty and students included strong objections to $3 million in University holdings in South African banks and other companies, where the oppression of blacks continued unchecked by the controlling government (Reilly, 1982, July 27, p. 1). A report spearheaded by a philosophy professor and issued by a University of Maine (Orono) faculty committee drew a 10-2 divestiture vote from The Board of Trustees (Reilly, p. 1). The featured statement within the report piqued the interest and concerns of Maine citizens:

> The University of Maine ought not to profit from the unique and morally reprehensible system of apartheid. There is a moral imperative to disassociate our university completely from the essential evil of apartheid. (Reilly, 1982, July 27, p. 1)

The divestiture decision took just three months to make.

Although Chancellor McCarthy always appeared to attract controversy, he lasted eleven years and was by far the State's longest serving chancellor. By many accounts, he spent the first several years putting out brush fires. In the early 1980s, however, trustees were ready to see a planning document finally emanate from his office, and there were indications that the Board may have pressured McCarthy with an upcoming performance assessment due upon the document's completion. McCarthy responded in a satisfactory manner, however, and he continued to serve the University System with an expanded role brought

4: Growth and Development of the System

about by the advent of a faculty union and the negotiating that its establishment entailed.

It was interesting to note at this juncture that the union's formation may have been precipitated by the Chancellor's actions, and that through the formation of the union, the role of chancellor became even more important, and the power of the office enhanced.

In 1983, Chancellor McCarthy suddenly announced that he would be resigning. The terms of the resignation, however, brought another bout of controversy to the University System. Once again, Maine people's attention focused on the Board of Trustees. From time to time over the history of the System, there were complaints raised by citizens, legislators, faculty, administrators, and others that the Board was too far removed from the day-to-day operations of the System and that, in addition, too much autonomy and decision-making power rested with them and the Office of Chancellor. A deal struck between the Board and the Chancellor upon the announcement of his resignation provided an example of this perception.

McCarthy and the Board announced that the Chancellor's resignation would include a one-year leave of absence to study at the John F. Kennedy School of Government in Cambridge, after which he would return to the University of Maine to become a fully tenured professor earning a salary that was approximately double that of the average faculty member's salary (Bailey, 1983, November 6, p. 15A). Not only was the salary issue on the minds of many of the faculty and other interested parties, but also the fact that the deal had been prearranged, apparently in secret, left some fuming (Bailey, p. 15A). It was difficult to discern whether tenure or salary angered the faculty more, but the union and the media made the tenure proposal an issue that the trustees could not ignore. McCarthy ended up withdrawing his resignation following the flap and indefinitely postponing a decision about when he might leave. He continued to preside through the formation of the Visiting Committee to the University of Maine, a committee that took the most comprehensive look ever at the University of Maine System and its future.

An attempt to change the System's organizational structure was spearheaded by Owen Wells, a Portland, Maine, lawyer and graduate of the System in 1984 (Himmelstein, 1983, December 4, p. 1). Although this attempt failed in the Maine Legislature, it was the first of many by

4: Growth and Development of the System

Wells to implement more than one Board of Trustees within the University of Maine System. In this initial attempt, Wells felt that the University of Southern Maine and the University of Maine at Orono should have their own boards, complete with full campus policymaking authority. His advocacy of a late 1990s proposal to restructure the System is also detailed later in this paper.

The University of Maine System hit a crossroads in the rancorous 1985-1986 academic year. In this highly charged period, major events included release of a controversial long-term plan from the trustees, the release of the "Visiting Committee Report to the University of Maine System," a major speech on the condition of higher education by outgoing Governor Joe Brennan, another request for the resignation of the trustees, the resignation of Chancellor McCarthy, and a debacle in which a new chancellor lasted just ten days.

The appointment of a Visiting Committee to the University of Maine by Governor Joseph Brennan put on hold any legislative attempts to change the structure of the system. Wells and his private group called the "Committee on Academic Excellence" were optimistic about what the Visiting Committee might recommend (Forkey, 1985, August 25, p. 19A). The Committee consisted of dignitaries and experts in higher education and public policy, and the members were well respected throughout Maine. Unfortunately for the System, the Board of Trustees had something else in mind.

The University of Maine Board of Trustees was long criticized for not involving themselves in planning processes that drew input from constituencies with an interest in the University of Maine System. They appeared to be either perplexed by the appointment of an independent visiting committee or pressured to propose something of value to right the perceived wrongs of public higher education in Maine. For whatever reason, trustees offered a new planning document entitled "The University and the Future" just weeks before the Visiting Committee released its own recommendations to the general public. Once again, reaction was extremely poor to the trustees' work, especially among legislators and editorial writers ("Big Plans," 1985, November 23, p. 22).

Having already announced that he would be finally leaving in 1986, it was not Chancellor McCarthy who took the brunt of the criticism this time around. Trustees were blasted across the state for composing their new planning document at a secretive retreat, allowing for no public

4: Growth and Development of the System

hearings or input, and for upstaging the Visiting Committee ("Big Plans," 1985, November 23, p. 22). The new goals were vague, other than to request an unprecedented $139 million in additional funds from the state, increasing the System's share of the state budget from 8 to 15 percent ("Big Plans," p. 22). Other stated goals included a reduction in undergraduate students of approximately eighteen hundred full-time students ("Big Plans," p. 22). The *Bangor Daily News* editorial staff complained about the trustees report's potential to de-emphasize the land-grant institution:

> ... some points raise serious doubts about UMO's future place in the system. One of them calls for 'assigning the regional undergraduate institutions the responsibility for undergraduate teacher preparation.' Another goal calls for continued development of 'the current mission of the University of Southern Maine as an urban graduate and undergraduate institution with the additional responsibility for providing baccalaureate programs in York County, Lewiston-Auburn, and Augusta.' Yet another calls for 'centralizing the direction of non-traditional two-year program mission of the University in Augusta and include such programs offered at all campuses.' ("Big Plans," 1985, November 23, p. 22)

Many others in the Orono/Bangor area scoffed at the trustees' report and bemoaned the timing. Just over one month later, the "Report of the Visiting Committee to the University of Maine" presented what some saw as polar opposite views from that of the trustees.

The Visiting Committee did see many similarities with that of the Board of Trustees. Each saw the System as containing important elements. For example, the report listed twenty recommendations that were highlighted by the System's need to consist of elements such as a research and doctoral university, an urban comprehensive university, and a group of regional baccalaureate colleges. The Board of Trustees agreed, but the reports had little more in common. The Visiting Committee's vision reflected a preeminent role for the Orono campus, and urged leaders to seriously improve their research and graduate opportunities. The Board's "University and the Future" report emphasized the University of Southern Maine's role as an urban comprehensive university, as well as moving to strengthen regional campuses at the expense of the land-grant institution. A majority of the members of the Maine Legislature clearly embraced the Visiting Committee Report over the board's plan (Rawson, 1986, January 15, p. 16).

In many ways, this bifurcated environment pitted the University of Maine's Orono campus, some legislators, editors, Visiting Committee members, and others against the remaining campus presidents and the Board of Trustees during the 1986 legislative session. The Legislature claimed university arrogance and demanded that the board endorse the Visiting Committee Report ("Umaine Growth," 1986, March 2, p. 17A). Things got so bad that Democrats and Republicans joined forces, and Republican House Minority Leader Thomas W. Murphy, a member of the Legislature's Joint Standing Committee on Education, challenged trustees to resign if they weren't capable and qualified (Rawson, 1986, January 15, p. 16). The struggle escalated, and was well represented by a *Maine Sunday Telegram* column entitled, "Legislature's View: University Arrogance," ("UMaine Growth," 1986, March 2, p. 17A). Consider the following:

> The University of Maine has not always been popular, either with the general public or its representatives in the state Legislature, over the past fifteen years. UM trustees are trying desperately to mend that relationship, which has so deteriorated that lawmakers, until last week, were considering a bill that would give the Legislature veto power over the trustees' choice of a chancellor to administer the system. ("UMaine Growth," 1986, March 2, p. 17A)

The move was the latest skirmish in years of growing frustration in the Legislature over what many lawmakers regard as the arrogance and isolation of the University's System's leadership ("UMaine Growth," p. 17A).

The President of the University of Southern Maine did his best to smooth over a difficult situation while favoring the trustee approach during February 1986. In a speech later published in the *Lewiston Sunday Sun*, Dr. Robert Woodbury highlighted the strengths of both reports, suggesting that the best of both be retained (Woodbury, 1986,

4: Growth and Development of the System

February 9, p. 3D). Dr. Woodbury, who soon would rise to become a chancellor for the University of Maine System, offered a detailed look at the proposals forwarded by both the board and the Visiting Committee. In defense of the board proposal, he offered the following:

> The strategic basis propounded by the Board of Trustees emerged from three years of data-gathering and reflection in which each campus participated. Whatever the political residue from the manner, form, and timing of the trustees' action, their effort essentially reaffirmed and endorsed the mission of USM as an urban comprehensive university with significant and growing responsibilities at the undergraduate and graduate level. The board also charged us with proposing the means and costs of baccalaureate-level programs more accessible to the citizens of Augusta, Lewiston/Auburn, and York County. (Woodbury, 1986, February 9, p. 3D)

Later in the same speech, Dr. Woodbury offered more specifics as to the weaknesses of the Visiting Committee's approach from a specific perspective relative to southern Maine:

> My concern is not that the committee addressed the realities and dreams of UMO, but that I do not believe it captured our reality and our dreams, to say nothing of the other campuses. The Visiting Committee could not do everything and we should not expect everyone else to see us as we might wish. But it is my conviction, after studying the report, that the committee did not fully grasp the nature of the southern Maine region and how it is changing. It did not appreciate the way in which comprehensive universities in populated areas across the nation have developed in response to the social, economic, and demographic changes over the past two decades; it did not understand our sense of how we have grown up and matured in quality over the decade; and it did not capture our vision of what a University of Southern Maine might be and is becoming in this region. Possibly we should not be surprised; we are complex and quite different in mission and character from more familiar and older models like a UMO or Bowdoin....As a consequence, the Visiting Committee

4: Growth and Development of the System

Report, for all its important strengths, does not proffer a vision of what USM might be in this region, in this state, and in this university fifteen years from now. (Woodbury, 1986, February 9, p. 3D)

The next chancellor would have to mend fences according to some legislators ("UMaine Growth," 1986, March 2, p. 17A). Although the next chancellor would not be Dr. Woodbury, he would become chancellor very soon, and with his thoughtful, pro-trustee, but somewhat contrary view to that of legislators, the job would be difficult. There was no question that Chancellor McCarthy would resign soon, as he had been preparing to for nearly three years. The only question was when; this was settled six months earlier than had been previously announced when McCarthy stepped aside in February 1986 rather than in September ("Chancellor McCarthy to Quit," 1985, July 23, p. 5).

The period between 1985 and 1986 may have done a great deal to promote the idea that there are "two Maines." The rural, agricultural Maine had been pitted against the urban and suburban needs of southern and coastal Maine for many years, and because the needs can be quite different between the two, problems occurred on economic, social, and political fronts. At this point in history, trustee membership was still dominated by individuals from southern parts of the state, a negative geographical factor that was carried over to Governor Brennan's term from Governor Longley's ("Balancing the Trustees," 1984, June 13, p. 14). Subsequently, rural legislators combined with coastal representatives--in effect, ganging up against increasingly isolated trustees--to support the rival Visiting Committee Report. This displaced some of the developing rural versus urban tension, transforming it to a different paradigm in the minds of many Mainers, in which specific members of the Board of Trustees represented an exclusivity of wealth, thought, and action. Those characteristics did not conform to blue-collar Maine or to their representatives in the Legislature.

Most legislators saw the Visiting Committee as a thoughtful and independent evaluator of the System. They had befriended personable committee members such as former Colby College president Robert Strider, Westbrook Hospital trustee Jean Childs, and Former U.S. Senator and Vice Presidential Candidate Edmund Muskie as leaders, constituents, and supporters. Conversely, feuds between legislators and trustees had been the norm and have continued throughout the history of the University of Maine System. During the same period that the board blamed inflation and under-funding from governors and legislators for most of the System's problems, they and the chancellor had approved fifty-six new academic programs (between 1975 and 1984). "We felt that in the desire to extend the benefits of education to everybody [the Board]...was in too great a rush to give a wide range of offerings," said Sills of the Visiting Committee ("UMaine Growth," 1986, March 2, p. 17A).

In a special report on the University of Maine entitled "UMaine Growth: Loose Controls, Planning" conducted by the *Maine Sunday Telegram*, blame was placed squarely on both the Board of Trustees and Chancellor McCarthy, echoing the conclusions in the Visiting Committee ("UMaine Growth," 1986, March 2, p. 17A). Shortages of classroom teachers, books and professional journals in the libraries, and modern equipment in the laboratories cut into the quality of the programs across the System, according to the newspaper account ("UMaine Growth," p. 17A). The telling list of shortcomings also laid blame on trustees, in that they:

- Failed to ensure the development of a formal academic plan for the System.
- Failed to insist on precise mission statements for the System's seven campuses.
- Failed to establish rigorous procedures for quality control of academic programs.
- Failed in their responsibility on the budget ("UMaine Growth," 1986, March 2, p. 17A).

In this climate, there was little reason to wonder why faculty had unionized.

The Visiting Committee's recommendations included calls to strengthen faculty by giving them "encouragement, financial and otherwise;" to "end reliance on tuition increases;" to allocate more funds to financial aid; and to provide support services in areas such as maintenance, replacement of equipment, clerical services to faculty, and providing laboratory supplies (Wilson, 1990, February 23, p. 14). All of these recommendations would cost money, and an additional $15 million legislative appropriation, along with the bond issue of 1986, did provide a jump-start. The most important factor was the appearance that the Visiting Committee provided a direction that had not existed in prior years. In conjunction with current campus missions and through a rededication to graduate scholarship at the Orono campus (as specified in the Visiting Committee Report), the System had the potential to regenerate. None of this would have happened were it not for the acceptance of the Visiting Committee by the general public. Trustees were in effect forced to endorse the components of its report.

Although Chancellor Freeman had no time to see its potential and future Chancellor Woodbury was slow to adopt its significance, the Visiting Committee's report helped higher education in Maine to become nationally competitive, especially at the Orono campus. By all accounts, the University of Southern Maine was the big loser, particularly in regard to the offering of research, graduate, and doctoral opportunities to the state's most heavily populated region.

The Administration of Governor Joseph E. Brennan (1979-1986)

Governor Joseph Brennan was simultaneously one of the most successful and one of the most unsuccessful political leaders in the history of Maine, if judged by the number of offices won and lost. He was never bashful about telling the people of Maine that he would like to serve them in public office, and more often than not he was successful. Beginning his career in the Maine House of Representatives in 1965, Joe Brennan has served as a District Attorney, Maine Attorney General, Maine State Senator, Congressman, and, finally, two terms as Governor of Maine from 1979 to 1986. He has also run and lost various bids for Governor and for United States Senator.

Governor Brennan entered the office during a period of harsh economic instability that lasted until his second term. In comparison to Governor John R. McKernan, Jr., who is discussed in the following chapter, Governor Brennan was slowly exposed to a strengthening economy. With an increasing budget to work with in his second term, Brennan was able to play a role in revitalizing the University of Maine System, mostly through the appropriations mechanism.

Governor Brennan changed the direction of the University System through the appointment of a Visiting Committee. In part, Governor Brennan's high-profile role was due not only to his personal interest in serving the educational needs of Maine, but also to good timing. During

4: Growth and Development of the System 79

the Brennan Administration, a public perception prevailed that academic quality was in serious decline. The historic educational report, "A Nation at Risk," prompted discussion across the country about the inadequacies of education from kindergarten through college (National Commission on Excellence in Education, 1983).

"A Nation at Risk" was not the only prompt for renewed attention. The University of Maine campus, located in Orono, had lost its Carnegie classification as a doctoral degree-granting institution in 1983 (State of Maine, 1986, p. 12). In addition, the problems in the Maine system of higher education, relative to the development of the economy, were the subject of a major report released in March 1982 entitled, "Planning for the 80s: Post-Secondary Education and the Maine Economy" (Mavrinac/Marsh Consultants & Mallar Development Services, Inc., 1982). The report was one of the first to defend higher education in Maine through the use of detailed statistics about the economic impact (i.e., ripple and multiplier effects). The total economic benefit of higher education in Maine was pegged at about $1.5 billion (Mavrinac/Marsh Consultants & Mallar Development Services, Inc., p. 1). Despite the recital of the numbers, public confidence sagged during the early 1980s.

Even the content within the "Planning for the 80s" report was unsettling. Field research from the report yielded the following observations about the interrelationship between industry and education:

> Despite a new orientation by public and independent post-secondary institutions toward the delivery of educational services, there is nonetheless *a serious and widening gap* between the post-secondary education world and the world of Maine production and service activities. It is a gap marked by an extensive sense on the part of entrepreneurs and employees that post-secondary institutions in the state, are, with a few exceptions, hardly relevant to their needs. It is a gap that if not reduced could seriously threaten the continued modernization of the Maine economy. (Mavrinac/Marsh Consultants & Mallar Development Services, Inc., 1982, p. 3)

The sentiment criticizing higher education repeated itself in the early 1990s under the McKernan Administration. Both the early 1980s and the early 1990s were characterized in Maine by a downward or stagnating economic environment and limited state resources. Poor economic circumstances led to quick criticism about what the University System was not doing well; during these periods, governors and legislatures were more apt to become involved. Higher education reform movements were taking center stage as a result of the perception of lower quality and insufficient or inadequate means of training and preparation for Maine's young people.

Governor Brennan took the offensive in his "State of the State Address" in 1983, recommending funding increases to both the University and Technical Colleges. Most important were his remarks that follow:

> But in a changing world...nothing is more certain...than that the future will belong to those who have the skills...that are needed in the marketplace.
> Tonight...therefore...I am recommending an 8 percent increase in what the state provides for local education. Tonight...I am very proud to recommend an appropriation of two million dollars...to establish a campus of the University of Maine at Lewiston...under the leadership of Mayor Paul Dionne. (Brennan, 1983, February 22, p. 8)

Governor Brennan continued to press the issue through the middle 1980s. In 1984, he created the Special Commission on the Condition of the Status of Education in Maine and chose Thomas Hedley Reynolds, the President of Bates College, to chair it (Brennan, 1984, January 31, p. 8). Governor Brennan also worked with the State Board of Education and the University of Maine System to create a new teacher's certification mechanism. Then, in 1985, Governor Brennan recommended a whopping 25 percent increase in funding for the University of Maine System over two years (Brennan, 1985, January 31, p. 6).

The focus on higher education in 1985 and previously accomplished work by Governor Brennan appeared to lead to a defining moment. Public expectations for higher education had rarely been lower. Governor Brennan's Special Commission on the Status of Maine Education toured the countryside, holding hearings that were dominated by "allegations of declining quality in the University" (State of Maine,

4: Growth and Development of the System 81

1986, p. 2). That group went on to recommend to the Governor and the Legislature that a special visiting committee be established. Thus, "The Report of the Visiting Committee to the University of Maine" may be one of the most referenced documents on higher education in the history of the state. Its recommendations were critical to the health of the University of Maine System, and they included statements on the structure of the system, the academic program, the governance and leadership of the system, and financial support (State of Maine, p. 21).

The twenty recommendations from the Visiting Committee went a long way toward strengthening the foundation of the University of Maine System. Recommendation Number Two (under the structural heading) may have been the most important. It recommended in no uncertain terms that the Orono campus "be strengthened as a research and doctoral institution," and that the "Carnegie classification of UMO as a doctoral institution...be restored" (State of Maine, 1986, p. 21). Restoration of the University of Maine's classification as a research and doctoral institution could not be achieved without a major commitment by the State. Recognizing this, Governor Brennan showed patience in January 1986 by declaring in his "State of the State Address" that, "We need not rush to pass judgment, or pass bills.....Haste would only cut short the wide-ranging and constructive dialogue that this report promises to generate" (Brennan, 1986, January 21, p. 9). Instead, the Governor waited until discussion cleared both the 1986 legislative session and trustee meetings. Other important reports and task forces internal to the University System were concurrently advancing recommendations, such as a report entitled "The University and the Future" (University of Maine System, 1985). This information, in the end, appeared to form a synthesis of many years of work, culminating in one of the most famous speeches ever delivered by any governor on the subject of higher education in Maine. An "Address on Higher Education" was delivered with fervor on March 20, 1986, in front of the One Hundred and Twelfth Maine Legislature, with most of the members of the Visiting Committee and other dignitaries in the field of higher education sitting in the balcony of the House Chamber. Most of the recommendations of the Visiting Committee were embraced, in one form or another. Governor Brennan declared the following:

Yes, the Maine people are the allies of University reform. The major enemy of reform is factionalism. It is the belief that what is good for the north is bad for the south. It is the belief that what is good for one campus is bad for another. It is the belief that what is good for business is bad for scholarship. Factionalism is an ancient human vice. President Abraham Lincoln once said, 'A house divided against itself cannot stand.' Our university system is one house--with many rooms, and with many campuses. Our university system cannot be divided against itself and still stand, and still do what the people of Maine need it to do.

...Today, I say to you that factionalism and divisiveness have no place in our debate, and have no place in any debate over something as important as higher education in Maine. (Brennan, 1986, March 20, p. 10)

Governor Brennan's commitment to higher education funding, along with an improving state and national economy under President Ronald Reagan, led to achievements that carried the University of Maine System into the remainder of the 1980s with a good financial foundation but a lot of unanswered questions.

The Term of Chancellor Jack E. Freeman (7/1/1986-7/16/1986)

Few chancellors in the United States have served a shorter term than Jack Freeman. Dr. Freeman, originally from Fort Worth, Texas, made a name for himself as an academic planner by devising creative ways to improve a five-campus University of Pittsburgh System (Garland, 1986, May 20, p. 2). He was credited with formulating many cost-saving plans while president at the University of Pittsburgh's Johnstown campus, including implementing a reduced-rate telephone system with a savings potential that totaled over $2.5 million per year, and financing other critical projects via tax-exempt bonding (Garland, p. 2). In addition, Dr. Freeman was instrumental in a move for the campus to self-insure with particular benefits to the medical college there (Garland, p. 2). With a stellar background in academic programming, planning, and financing, the Board of Trustees of the University of Maine System felt strongly that Freeman was the best person for the job. His doctorate in higher education administration was well coupled with a master's degree in political science from Baylor University and his experience as an

4: Growth and Development of the System 83

assistant professor of political science at the U.S. Air Force Academy (Garland, p. 2). Hired in May after Maine's rancorous spring of 1986, which saw the "Report of the Visiting Committee to the University of Maine" and the controversial, poorly received planning document entitled "The University and the Future," the Board of Trustees felt strongly that Freeman was the man who could lead the System toward a brighter future.

Whether the trustee's assessment was correct will never be known due to yet another statewide controversy. Trustees set the Chancellor's salary at $114,000 per year, with a $12,000 housing allowance and many other benefits (Garland, 1986, May 20, p. 1). The salary was $35,000 higher than McCarthy's (who had held the post for eleven years), and $40,000 more than the State's highest paid public official (Garland, 1986, May 21, p. 7).

The attacks on trustees were immediate and prolonged. State Senator John Baldacci of Bangor, who would later rise to become a Democratic congressman from Maine's Second District, touched off the firestorm. Baldacci ignited the criticism by immediately sending a letter to trustee Chair Joseph G. Hakanson calling the salary decision "boldly insensitive to Maine taxpayers" (Forkey, 1986, June 9, p. 1). The Bangor State Senator went on to say that he was "astounded and outraged by your proposal to catapult the chancellor's salary almost 50 percent....I look forward to your justification to Maine taxpayers and students who will be footing the bill if this salary is approved" (Garland, 1986, May 20, p. 1). Following the letter's publicity, others joined in. State Representative Ada Brown, House Chair of the Legislature's Education Committee, predicted that voters would reject a proposed $7.7 million bond issue slated for the coming November 1986 elections (Forkey, p. 1). Porter D. Leighton, a candidate for the Republican nomination for governor in the June primaries, also said he was "outraged," while his primary opponent and later victorious Republican nominee John R. McKernan, Jr., supported the trustees' decision (Forkey, p. 1).

Trustee David Flanagan publicly defended his fellow board members' decision. "What I'm looking for from Dr. Freeman is that he prove to be cost effective....I think Dr. Freeman can get these doors open," said Flanagan, citing the new Chancellor's experience. Mathematics Professor Clayton Dodge agreed in an open letter to the *Bangor Daily News*, stating that Freeman would be "worth every penny

84   4: Growth and Development of the System

if he will do the job effectively"--despite admitting that the $35,160 salary increase was more than he made annually after thirty years with the University of Maine (Forkey, 1986, June 9, p. 1).

Although McKernan would later rise to become Governor, the political momentum never turned in favor of the new Chancellor. A telling blow occurred before July 1, the first day in which Freeman took office. Gil Rogers, president of the Associated Faculties of the University of Maine, weighed in by claiming that if the trustees were willing to enter the top of the national market for administrators, then they ought to be willing to raise faculty pay, which ranked forty-fourth lowest in the nation at that time (Garland, 1986, May 21, p. 7).

The headlines rang out on July 17, 1986. "Disillusioned Chancellor Quits" was the front-page story in the *Portland Press Herald* (Forkey, 1986, July 17, p. 1). A letter written by the exiting Chancellor to Governor Joe Brennan, serving out his final year in office, explained the problem in great detail:

> After two weeks of intensive review of the financial and academic condition of the System, and the political and economic climate in Maine, I have reluctantly concluded that the high goals enunciated by the Visiting Committee and endorsed by the Board are probably not attainable within the resources likely to be available now and in the future. I, frankly, am disillusioned by the general climate of public opinion in Maine in respect to the University System, as manifested in the public outcry over my salary, and that of Dr. Lick; the threats from some quarters to 'punish' the Board and the University by denying approval of a badly needed, quite modest, and fully justifiable bond issue; and the intense politicization of even minor issues at the University. (Forkey, 1986, July 17, p. 1)

The full text of the resignation letter written by Freeman to Governor Brennan is in Appendix B of this book. Dr. Lick, referenced previously, was the President of the University of Maine.

Freeman was thought to be referring to Senator Baldacci and other members of the Maine Legislature throughout his letter. Trustee Chair Hakanson said that Freeman felt the Orono campus did not have a "fighting chance" to be brought up to the quality level envisioned by the

4: Growth and Development of the System

Visiting Committee, and that there were "just so many problems politically and throughout the state, he felt it was best for him to resign" (Forkey, 1986, July 17, p. 1). Hakanson continued: "The essence of what he was driving at is that we had a mandate from the Visiting Committee and endorsed by practically everyone to achieve some high goals for the University," and that reaching those goals meant "faculty, number one, and administration, number two" (Forkey, p. 1).

From the union to the legislature to university employees to the people of Maine, it seemed that everyone was grumbling about who was responsible for the whole mess. Freeman himself did not leave unscathed. *Lewiston Sun Journal* editorial writers complained that Freeman's sudden departure "smacks of unprofessionalism for an individual to assume the important position of university chancellor at a high salary and then leave it before making an effort to tackle the problems of the institution" ("Freeman Resignation," 1986, July 18, p. 6A).

Regardless of which party should have the most blame laid at its doorstep, Freeman's resignation and the condition of the University at that time left the University of Maine System vulnerable. Trustees knew that a new chancellor would have to be chosen quickly, and were forced to admit that the Visiting Committee Report envisioned the best possible outcome for Maine higher education. Even following Freeman's resignation there would be further attacks on the Board of Trustees, including new salary and payment flaps, suggestions that legislators should play a role in appointing the next chancellor, and demands that the hiring process for a new chancellor be known to the public.

The Third Phase: 1987-2000

The final phase to be explored is dominated by two major figures. Chancellor Robert L. Woodbury, arguably the most effective chancellor in the System's history, teamed with Governor John R. McKernan to create an effective one-two punch over a seven-year period. Unfortunately, these men experienced both the best and the worst of economic times during their tenures. In addition, the odd but interesting reign of Chancellor J. Michael Orenduff and the quiet tenure of Governor Angus S. King are documented here. Maine's most recent chancellor, Terrence MacTaggart, brought an intellectual approach and a keen understanding of the impact of systemic structural properties to the state.

The Term of Chancellor Robert L. Woodbury (1986-1993)

In many ways, Dr. Robert Woodbury represented the nexus between what the University of Maine System once was and what it was to become, not just because of the leadership from the new chancellor, but also because of the impact of the Visiting Committee report. The report's impact was felt from an operations standpoint, to be sure, but more importantly, the document has served as an historical reference point for that which has gone right and that which has gone wrong within the System. The year of 1986 proved to be a pivotal one for the System; rather than come apart at the seams, as many predicted, the University climate would gradually improve until about 1990.

Dr. Woodbury had displayed his public relations talents as a president within the System at the University of Southern Maine. It would be necessary to draw upon all of his skills and more if he were to be able to bring the System from its state of disarray in August 1986 toward a collective vision of what it could and should be.

Would his ability to carry out a collective vision be compromised by his prior adherence to the unpopular trustee proposals of late 1985? This speculation is refuted in this research. Nevertheless, it appeared to be a factor considered by trustees in their choice of the new chancellor. By way of law, it was the trustees who would decide who the next chancellor would be, and Woodbury's relationship with them was obviously solid. He was rewarded with their confidence and appointed quite quickly following the Freeman debacle.

In the month prior to his appointment, some must have wondered if the Maine Legislature itself would be taking on the responsibilities of running the University of Maine System. Following State Senator Baldacci's criticisms of the prior chancellor's salary, he and others continued their active public roles, to the ire of many in the higher education community. Baldacci publicly proposed that former Governor Kenneth M. Curtis be given the job, and he recommended Curtis to a member of the newly revived search committee (Garland, 1986, July 24, pp. 1-2). This action raised a lot of eyebrows and led to speculation that the University's agency structure might be changed in the next legislative session after all.

An account by the *Bangor Daily News* stated that Baldacci felt no guilt when former Chancellor Freeman listed the salary controversy as a reason for his departure (Garland, 1986, July 24, p. 2). Other legislators

4: Growth and Development of the System

raised a new issue of a $4,700 payment that was made to Chancellor Freeman for his two weeks worth of work. John Diamond, House minority leader, wrote to the ex-chancellor requesting that he do the following:

> ...return to the University any compensation you have or will receive for your ten days in office.....If this cannot be resolved...undoubtedly, the outrage over the salary and your departure will spill over onto the next chancellor and inhibit our ability to put together a system of higher education as great as the University of Maine can and should be. (Garland, 1986, July 24, p. 2)

A pre-paid housing allowance of $1,000 was returned (Garland, 1986, July 24, p. 2). It is interesting to note that a few years later, Diamond would become the Director of Public Affairs at the University of Maine's Orono campus.

In the month prior to the Woodbury appointment, other legislators moved to demand that the Board of Trustees appear in front of the Legislature's Education Committee to answer questions about the candidates and the process, which various accounts indicated were again shrouded in secrecy (Garland, 1986, July 24, p. 2). The legislative antics finally provoked Trustee Francis Brown to vent his frustrations. A portion of a *Bangor Daily News* account describes the environment:

> Trustee Francis Brown responded that it's 'embarrassing' when legislators 'with two or three years under their belt' think they can run the University better than trustees. University of Maine trustees should be able to concentrate on getting a new chancellor and 'not think they have to pacify legislators who see an opportunity to kick a downed dog,' he added....Brown refused to call the hearing and criticized some legislators, 'who have patterned themselves after Speaker (John) Martin in terms of intimidating. They are abusing the power entrusted to them,' Brown said. (Garland, 1986, July 24, p. 2)

Baldacci responded by expressing an interest in resurrecting the bill to examine the university structure when the legislature was to reconvene in December 1986 and by complaining that the new search process was being rushed (Garland, 1986, August 6, 1986, p. 1). He felt that Governor Curtis or Acting Chancellor Harlan Phillipi would make good chancellors, and he stated that he did not understand "why we have to look much further than in our midst" (Garland, 1986, July 24, p. 2). He was apparently deflated and politically embarrassed with the surprise response from the press that neither man wanted the job (Garland, p. 2). It appeared that Baldacci had not checked in with those whom he recommended. Baldacci concluded by suggesting that an interim appointment should be made in case legislators decide restructuring is needed (Garland, p. 2). This request exemplified peak legislative interference.

For the most part, trustees ignored legislators who would have chosen to appoint the new chancellor themselves, but apparently they did feel the heat. According to the minutes of August 25, 1986, Woodbury beat out another Maine resident, Richard Barringer, becoming chancellor for a salary of $96,000, with no housing allowance (Board of Trustees of the University of Maine System, 1986, August 25, p. 1). The desire to have the appointment filled by a familiar Mainer, along with the housing-allowance controversy, certainly played a role in this decision. However, Mainers once again felt betrayed by the board when it moved in a $1,000 monthly housing allowance to Woodbury just three months later (Board of Trustees of the University of Maine System, 1986, November 24, p. 8).

Despite the intense pressure, the new chancellor briskly attempted to save the $7.7 million bond issue that he saw as a critical step toward modernization (Garland, 1986, October 23, p. 20). He spearheaded a media and advertising blitz that appeared mostly to rely on free publicity.

The bond issue succeeded. It provided a library computer research mechanism that was state-of-the-art. Woodbury and Dale Lick, the controversial president of the University of Maine, envisioned a local and regional system of connected databases that would eventually evolve into the broad-based Internet-related concepts of the new millennium. It was a move that, combined with other technological investments, vaulted Maine into the cutting edge of communications technology and drew interest in business applications in the field.

4: Growth and Development of the System

The final years of the decade of the 1980s were very productive for the System. Comparatively, the University of Maine System flourished--financially, academically, and socially. It gained critical strength under Woodbury's watch. State appropriations and charitable giving grew, although the balance of the University's budget still relied too heavily on state dollars. A 1987 document entitled "Internal Review and Assessment of Development Capabilities" provided some hope that the criticism by the Visiting Committee over poor efforts in the private philanthropy might soon be put to rest (State of Maine, 1986, p. 9). An over-emphasis on athletics and tuition and an under-emphasis on the community college concept began to worry faculty, but the economic good times of the late 1980s muted many concerns.

In 1987, Governor McKernan proposed $55 million in new funds for the biennial budget, including increases in state appropriations in fiscal years 1987 and 1988 that were the highest percentage increases in the nation (McKernan, 1989, January, p. 15). Woodbury played a significant role in lobbying for the dollars. Trustee management of the new influx of state funds was troubling, however, in that despite a $15 million supplemental appropriation and the highest enrollment in the history of the University of Maine, a 5 percent across-the-board tuition hike was passed in July 1987 (Board of Trustees of the University of Maine System, 1987, July 20, p. 4). Tuition and new mandatory student fees would be the revenue source of choice among trustees who were beginning to be criticized for these practices. In a March 1987 meeting of the board, for example, several students attended the meeting to ask trustees not to implement a new mandatory student life fee at the Orono campus (Board of Trustees of the University of Maine System, 1987, March 26, p. 1). Yet, the trustees moved to assess the $100 per student fee at the same meeting (Board of Trustees of the University of Maine System, p. 7).

The growth pattern of the University System was also problematic in the pivotal years of the late 1980s. Again, it was difficult for any university advocate to register complaints during such good economic times. But in January 1988, there were some rumblings. As was reported previously, trustees endorsed the Visiting Committee's report following great public pressure to abandon their own long-term plan. The Visiting Committee had recommended concentrating efforts on the health of the land-grant campus; for the most part, the System achieved great success

4: Growth and Development of the System

in returning the Orono campus to a position of respectability as an accredited center for graduate and undergraduate scholarship. Unfortunately, in doing so, it was the urban comprehensive campus at the University of Southern Maine that suffered from weak support. On January 25, 1988, a comparative study of the University of Southern Maine with other similar institutions revealed that USM "lags in breadth and depth of program offerings, especially at the graduate levels" (Board of Trustees of the University of Maine System, 1988, January 25, p. 4). The University of Southern Maine was clearly not engaged in looking for niches in graduate work that could be offered to the vast population of the southern Maine region.

The early 1990s were dominated by an economy that was weakening considerably. The significant problem for Woodbury involved what to do about the flattening level of funding. Serious tuition increases were necessitated when Chancellor Woodbury and the trustees told Governor McKernan that the System would not be able to meet McKernan's budget-reduction targets (Norton, 1990, December 11, p. 1A). As stated in the section on Governor McKernan's tenure, undergraduate tuition rose by 10.5 percent between 1989 and 1995, and the number of full-time equivalent university employees was cut by 9.4 percent (University of Maine System, 1995, pp. 4 and 7). In 1990, Chancellor Woodbury was in the midst of implementing a $9.6 million cut and deferments and freezes across the decision-making spectrum (Allen, 1990, December 16, p. 1D). State government had started the 1990-1991 academic year off on the wrong foot by having to delay a payment to the University System due to insufficient funds (Perry, 1990, August 1, p. 3). Morale was cited as a problem by many faculty who were venting most of their frustration on campus presidents, especially Dale Lick of Orono (Reilly, 1990, November 29, p. 1). The morale and overall climate at Orono began to decline in the spring of 1990 and continued into the 1990-1991 academic year. Residential-life employees were the first to feel the budget axe with layoffs, and more were contemplated at the University of Maine campus (Curran, 1990, June 27, p. 7). A five-year athletics plan for the flagship campus that had been developed and implemented by Woodbury and President Lick was strong, especially in support of the gender equity principles contained in federal law (Dowd, 1990, May 22, p. 1). But the feeling on campus was that the athletic department was left unaffected by the State and University revenue shortfall, and the resentment in

4: Growth and Development of the System

Orono grew. While Maine philanthropist Harold Alfond's donation of $2 million for a new arena was cheered, an undercurrent of jealousy boiled in faculty who had travel budgets eliminated and supplies reduced.

President Lick encountered most of the negativism at the Orono campus. At the same time that Woodbury's efforts were being praised by legislators in Augusta, Lick was receiving some major blows (Perry, 1990, February 11, p. 1). The complaints, too numerous to cover in entirety, included a perceived overemphasis on athletics, excessive administrative buildup, an insensitive racial comment, the mishandling of a sex scandal involving a women's basketball coach, and running up departmental budget deficits at the University of Maine (Perry, p. 1). An audit conducted by State Auditor Rodney L. Scribner caused concern about the administrative buildup at the Orono campus, which Scribner said rose by 13.3 percent from 1986 to 1989, while the student population rose by just 5.2 percent (Perry, p. 1). One legislator deadpanned that morale can be easily hurt when faculty are told that they cannot attend professional conferences, while at the very same time the baseball team conducts spring training in Hawaii (Perry, p. 1). Probably the most damaging event of all, however, was the following comment by Lick himself: "...research shows that there are several sports where black athletes are just naturally better [than whites]" (Perry, p. 1). The racial overtones of that statement caused a media explosion and eventually contributed to the downfall of President Lick.

Woodbury admitted that Lick's comments displayed insensitivity, but defended Lick for other administrative decisions that were, for the most part, authorized by trustees. Lick returned the volley to caviling legislators:

> People see us doing well (in sports)...they see Dale Lick cheering the team on television and they draw the conclusion that Dale Lick is giving all his money to athletics. It simply isn't true....We've been asked to do a lot of things. We need people...I've made decisions. We've moved forward. [But] when you've got people on the outside telling you what to do when they don't have the facts and don't understand the educational environment, sometimes you've got to say no. (Perry, 1990, February 11, p. 1)

A nationally competitive record was the reward to the University of Maine and to the other Maine campuses for the support of athletics over the years. Unfortunately, the good years of the 1980s and 1990s that were accentuated by national championship appearances were also tarnished by sex scandals, student-led gambling rings, mismanagement of athletic eligibility, and coaching suspensions. Nevertheless, the University of Maine ran up an impressive list of achievements, championships, and even some successful professional athletes.

Woodbury was soon forced to seriously downsize the System, but not without a fight. In 1991, Woodbury followed the lead of past chancellors by suggesting that the legislature consider a tax increase to help fund the needs of the University System. Some statements in an annual speech to state legislators drew interest, such as the following: "Compare, just for a moment, the annual expense of maintaining citizens in poverty or a correctional institution, with the education of a citizen to become a productive taxpayer" (Hale, 1991, April 26, p. 1). But in one of the worst economic periods in years, state revenues were nowhere to be found and the comparison he asked legislators to make hardly lasted for the moment for which he asked. Dr. Woodbury was later questioned about whether he supported a tax increase to generate new revenues to replace a proposed cut of $30 million. His answer of yes was rejected by the legislature, at least in terms of sending new money via taxation to the University of Maine System (Hale, p. 1).

The flagship campus at Orono took the brunt of the cuts, which ran counter to the Visiting Committee recommendations. The cuts of 1990 and 1991 were not as bad as had been anticipated, though, due to high tuition increases approved by the trustees, $3 million in reduced faculty salaries, and some additional last-minute State appropriations (Norton, 1991, July 21, p. 1B). Legislators were heard to say that System leaders' cried wolf and "over-dramatized their needs at times" (Norton, p. 1B). Faculty complained that the reliance on raising tuition and limiting faculty salaries was "the worst kind of planning because decisions aren't being driven by your priorities" (Norton, p. 1B). But in those dark days of shrinking public resources, and given the breadth of program commitments, most found praise for Chancellor Woodbury.

A ten-year plan entitled "Project 2002" emphasized excellence in undergraduate education and greater access to graduate programs (Brewer, 1992, August 5, p. 7A). According to Chancellor Woodbury,

4: Growth and Development of the System

it would serve as a "catalyst for creative action throughout the system" (Brewer, p. 7A). It was believed that the planning document would lead to stronger collaborations between campuses and local school systems, as well as a more suitable emphasis at the University of Maine and the University of Southern Maine on graduate education (Brewer, p. 7A). Little successful long-term planning had been noted since 1972 and, in general, this was the first long-term plan spawning from a chancellor and board that avoided major criticism. An emphasis on long-term planning was thought to be long overdue.

Robert Woodbury announced in April 1993 that he would be stepping down by September of that year, giving trustees the necessary time to search for a replacement (Troyer, 1993, April 23, p. 1A). In addition to initiatives already mentioned, he was credited with assisting in the development of an interactive educational television network, promoting new agreements and relationships with the American University in Bulgaria, and fostering better cooperation between campuses and their missions (Troyer, p. 1A). Woodbury's quiet leadership style would prove to be greatly missed, especially when later compared to his successor, the controversial J. Michael Orenduff.

The Administration of Governor John R. McKernan, Jr. (1987-1994)

Like Governor Joseph Brennan, Governor John R. McKernan, Jr., served previously in the Maine State Legislature and in the United States Congress before he took over as Chief Executive in 1987. From the outset, Governor McKernan's goal was to be known as a pro-education governor. He cared deeply for education and strove to provide a wider variety of educational services to Maine citizens. During his tenure, he created new programs and strengthened existing ones that sought to reach out to average and below-average Maine students. His "Human Resource Development Plan of 1988" was goal-oriented and focused on measurable strategies in the areas of job training and retraining, and in other strategies "for helping youth make the transition from school to work" (State of Maine, 1988, July 1, p. 64). The progress of the University of Maine System that he witnessed in the middle 1980s allowed him to stay on course through provision of increasing university appropriations, while at the same time developing a deeper commitment to secondary school-to-work programs and school-to-post-secondary transition strategies. In a relatively short period of time, his school-to-work strategies became successful national models. During his tenure, he privatized the Jobs for Maine's Graduates program (J.M.G.), in the process making it the most recognized school-to-work program of its kind in the United States. The J.M.G. program targeted underprivileged youths in secondary education, concentrated on getting kids back into high school, and focused on a specific career path and training. His long-term objective with this population was that if young people could neither complete high school nor focus on a job, they would quickly enter the welfare system and never be able to aspire to high wages or higher education of any kind. The preventative focus took hold in Maine and is still expanding today. Focused strategies helping youths who came from different economic, social, and academic backgrounds were McKernan's passion. He envisioned a more flexible system of life-long learning that would accentuate access as the ultimate outcome.

The Maine Youth Apprenticeship Program (later renamed Maine Career Advantage) was designed as a partnership among higher education, secondary schools, businesses, and government, according to McKernan's book entitled *Making the Grade* (McKernan, 1994). The program was very different than the J.M.G. initiative. It offered an alternative for young people that allowed them to enter the program in the last two years of high school and receive an apprenticeship from a participating area business. In addition, the first year of tuition in the Maine Technical College (or, in a few cases, the University of Maine) would be waived. In essence, McKernan believed that the University of Maine System and the Technical College System were prepared to accept Maine's best and brightest, but that there were grave weaknesses in servicing other student populations. Governor McKernan sought to address these populations.

In an oral interview following his final term as Governor, McKernan reflected on the type of students who he believed could receive a better education with the more specialized philosophy:

> The important thing, though, that we're trying to stress is that the history of education in this country really centered around either the best students or the worst students. And the reason is that the kids in the middle were always able to get a decent job when they got out of school, even if they didn't have much formal education. And that's what has changed in our society.

4: Growth and Development of the System 95

We have become so technology-driven, and the competition from outside America is so great, that we are now requiring more and more skills in our work force. And it's that great middle, which has sort of been ignored as they move through the education system because they didn't cause problems and they weren't going to go to four-year colleges--so as long as they make it through and got the basics, they could do fine with the kind of jobs that we had in our country. That has changed; therefore, our schools have to change. I think the only way they can do that is if businesses get involved in helping them establish what criteria they need in order to be able to hire kids coming out of the schools during the last part of the 1990s and the beginning of the twenty-first century. That's going to be important, no matter what part of the country you come from (Novak, 1995, pp. 2-3).

Governor McKernan goes on in the interview to interrelate his concept of serving all populations of students in their efforts toward life-long learning. In addressing a question about the problem that some states were having in transferring two-year and technical-college credits into four-year universities, he further developed his commitment to variety in educational opportunity:

Well, we have a little bit of a problem with that, too, especially in the two-year to four-year situation. But we have a very good chancellor of our university system who believes strongly that a four-year education is not in everybody's best interest. I didn't appoint him, by the way, but he agrees with my view that what we need to do is make sure we offer a lot of options so that people get to play to their strengths. It may be a one-year certificate for some people, or it may be a two-year or a four-year degree. But what we need to do is have those options available and make sure they are interrelated pathways so you can get credit for the path that you've taken, if you decide you want to move onto another one. That is really the underpinnings on which our program is based. (Novak, 1995, p. 5)

4: Growth and Development of the System

Governor McKernan's persistence in philosophy and implementation earned him the School-to-Work Transition Award from the National Alliance of Business. He also has served as the chairman of the Jobs for America's Graduates Program, the national school-to-work transition program of which Maine is the most prominent member. McKernan's passion was the success of the average student, and he probably contributed more to this group than many other Maine governors.

Another major initiative during the McKernan Administration was the emergence of public policy think tanks from within the University of Maine and the University of Southern Maine. The Governor was interested in academic leaders within the universities becoming more involved in the shaping of public policy. In a paper presented to the 1997 LINKS Conference (an annual national conference promoting stronger ties between state policymakers and higher education), Steve Ballard, Director of The University of Maine's Margaret Chase Smith Center for Public Policy, describes the initial development of what was then called the Maine Partnership Program:

> The Partnership Program was created to formally link two of the state's largest institutions at the research level. It was influenced by two nearly simultaneous occurrences. In 1987, Governor McKernan and Bob Woodbury, Chancellor of the University of Maine System, agreed to the importance of the idea for better linkages. Funding for the program, entitled the State Government/University of Maine System Partnership Program, would be provided jointly by the Governor's office and the Office of the Chancellor, with each committing $20,000 per year. A director and one staff member were hired in the spring of 1989 and the program formally began in the fall of 1989. A search of other states was conducted and no comparable models were found, at least at the Governor-Chancellor level. Hence, the program was created from scratch during its first year. (Ballard, 1997, p. 14)

Eventually, this program led to the Board of Trustee's establishment of the Margaret Chase Smith Center for Public Policy at the University of Maine, and the Muskie Institute at the University of Southern Maine, "both primarily intended to provide applied research, education, and

4: Growth and Development of the System

public service to the State of Maine (Ballard, 1997, p. 14). Although state funding dried up during the recession of the 1990s, public-policy think tanks were here to stay, "serving state needs rather than academic priorities" (Ballard, p. 15). Funding for think tanks in the 1990s slowly shifted from the state to the university and university-orchestrated grant activity, and the independent budget of these centers became compromised. More on the tightening university control of policy institutes is detailed in the section on secondary literature trends of the 1990s.

Another strength of the McKernan Administration during his first term in the public-policy arena was the successful guidance of a major bond issue through the legislative branch and public referenda process. The most substantial bond issue in decades allocated millions for the construction and upgrading of libraries, classrooms, laboratories, and other educational facilities at all branches of the University of Maine system. Memories of the early bond issue failures of the 1970s quickly faded. In 1987, Governor McKernan also proposed $55 million in new funds for the biennial budget, "to provide the quality education necessary for the future prosperity of our citizens and our state" (McKernan, 1987, February 5, p. 7).

Governor McKernan's funding increases to the University of Maine System during his first term peaked in 1989-1990. Unfortunately, economic circumstances seriously curtailed financial support from 1990 to 1994, leading Maine public higher education to retrenchment strategies and sharp tuition increases. At the height of the prosperity, generally recognized as the fiscal year 1988-1989, McKernan zeroed in on improving public access. In his 1989 "State of the State Address," he underscored the commitment:

> We are proposing to consolidate all of our student aid programs within one Higher Education Authority that will offer "one-stop shopping" to students, parents, and guidance counselors seeking financial-aid assistance information. Within that Authority, we intend to create a loan program of last resort in order to make it crystal clear to everyone in this state that, as far as this administration is concerned, no eligible Maine student is going to be denied access to higher education solely due to an inability to pay. (McKernan, 1989, January 26, pp. 13-14)

Governor McKernan's efforts in the 1980s did not prevent the often-discussed 1990s problem of the low number of Maine citizens that complete college degrees. Nevertheless, without his efforts, it is likely that Maine citizens would have been further relegated to a greatly inferior position.

Without question, then, the final four years of the 1980s represented the best of times for the University of Maine System. Even in these fruitful years, there were a few problems, however. The most notable issues were raised in a report completed for the University of Maine System entitled "Review and Assessment of Development Capabilities" (Ketchum, 1987). The report outlined real shortcomings in the ability of the System to aggressively raise funds from private sources. With such a critical shortcoming, the impending recession would have an even more devastating impact on the campuses. Inadequacy was the word, according to the report:

> ...To one degree or another, the campuses have not maximized their fund-raising potential. The primary reasons for the conditions are as follows:
> A - There has been significant turnover at the Presidential level and at key development and administrative posts.
> B - There is a wide assumption that alumni of means are not available.
> C - There is a reluctance to involve business on a local level.
> D - There has been a lack of budget and seasoned, professional staff.
> E - The level of cooperation among competing fund-raising interests on campuses - foundation, alumni, development, etc. - has been almost non-existent. (Ketchum, 1987, p. 3)

The high level of dependence on state spending, combined with poor internal fund-raising efforts and an oncoming economic downturn, was a recipe for disaster in Governor McKernan's second term. It did not happen all at once but, over time, public higher education would suffer. Beginning in the early 1990s, the general focus of debate in higher education literature in Maine turned to financing. A big change took place in 1990. As Maine's economy soured, so did the significant

4: Growth and Development of the System

increases in funding that had characterized the late 1980s. By the time the "Report of the Commission to Assess the Impact of Increased State Spending on the University of Maine System" (1990) was completed, there was little time to worry about further spending increases or what to do about them (State of Maine, 1990). Governor McKernan clearly did not know just how bad things would get when in 1990 he said, "We face a daunting challenge as the economy slows, but I know we will not fail" (McKernan, 1990, January 25, p. 26). Two years later, the economic devastation hollowed his words further:

> These are drastically different questions from those you have asked in other sessions. The economist John Denneth Galbraith once said that politics is the art of choosing between the disastrous and the unpalatable. As unpalatable as these choices may be for many of you, they pale in comparison to the personal anguish you will cause if you fail to act. (McKernan, 1992, p. 22)

To make things worse, many in the business world criticized academia's approach during this period, and their faith in the traditional college and university approach will be difficult to improve. For example, consider the following comments that appeared in "Small Business Forum" (1990) by David S. Krause, a nationally known businessman and consultant:

> Here's how an academic could help me: he or she could come to my factory at 6 a.m. and give me an honest day's worth of work on the shop floor! ...I do not believe that the modern corporate management theories taught by business school faculty apply as well to small firms as they do to large corporations. Additionally, I believe that professors overall do not possess enough real-world experience to fully grasp what small-business owners need to understand. (Krause, Sloan, Jagerman, Bernier, Katz, Kuratko & Engeleiter, 1990, p. 1)

Work-force issues, business needs, technological changes, demographic trends, distance learning, athletics, and the role of research all appeared as major components in the period's literature on higher education in Maine. Probably the most significant problem that surfaced revolved around what to do about the flattening level of funding coming from the State's general fund budget. With State resources to the University of Maine System remaining constant in total dollars, tuition levels rose quickly. The cumulative percentage change in the University of Maine System's appropriation coming from the State's general fund dropped by 3.5 percent in the period between 1989 and 1995 (University of Maine System, 1995, p. 3). During the same period, undergraduate tuition rose by 10.5 percent (University of Maine System, p. 4). In addition, the number of full-time equivalent education-related employees was cut by 9.4 percent (University of Maine System, p. 7).

These trends caused many reactions by leading educators and other advocates throughout the period. For example, in 1992, Chancellor Robert Woodbury observed the following: "Public higher education has taken a highly disproportionate share of cuts in State spending...only four states in the nation took larger cuts than Maine" (Woodbury, 1992, p. 5). These factors and others compelled Woodbury to make the following remark in his 1993 "State of the University of Maine System Address":

> "Even if recent budget cuts had been less lethal, the fiscal structure of the public sector at both the federal and state levels *and* the convulsive changes occurring in our society impel us to rethink how we function and what we do. (Woodbury, 1993, p. 3)

One example that shaped Woodbury's "rethinking" was an ongoing proposal to "downsize" the flagship institution at Orono, as well as make other system-wide adjustments. Orono Campus President Frederick Hutchinson offered "The University of Maine Preliminary Downsizing Proposal" on April 15, 1993 (Hutchinson, 1993). In many ways, this working document became a representation of the tough fiscal times and, in addition, a sagging confidence in the University of Maine's system, structure, governance, and leadership. The University of Maine flagship campus prepared the proposal to "downsize" based on the President's review of "the expectations of the people of Maine, whose tax dollars help support us and who look to us for leadership in enhancing the quality and conditions of life" (Hutchinson, 1993, p. 1).

4: Growth and Development of the System

Unfortunately for the University System, other controversies continued to take a toll, and Maine's public higher education system was severely jolted by these controversies. These problems included faculty resistance to degree-granting on interactive television; the role, level, and appropriateness of athletics at the flagship institution; a one-year, self-imposed suspension of the University of Maine hockey coach, who once won a national championship and returned to win another in 1999; official National Collegiate Athletic Association sanctions at the land-grant campus, which included a suspension and probationary period, as well as a loss of athletic scholarships; long labor disputes with faculty and staff; a persistent inability to transfer academic credits between System institutions; the controversial return of one million dollars to the State by the Chancellor's office to bolster sagging state coffers; and, most importantly, an unprecedented vote of no confidence in the Chancellor by the System's faculty. The cumulative effect of all these events carried well into the administration of Governor Angus S. King, Jr.

These problems, along with the economic stagnation that characterized the period, changed the view of many Maine citizens regarding the effectiveness of higher education. There is little argument that job-oriented technical training received a big boost during the 1990s, possibly at the expense of the University of Maine System.

Reports that followed maintained the theme of the economic boom turned to bust. The report entitled "Positioning the University of Maine System for the Twenty-first Century: Project 2002" heavily emphasized the application of economies of scale and long-term financing that would "avoid 'boom and bust budget cycles'" (Board of Trustees of the University of Maine System, 1992, p. 2). More sentiments from Chancellor Woodbury during his "State of the University System Address" in 1993 reflected the stark realization of the times and the attitude of a public struggling to deal on its own with the recession:

> Every day, of course, I receive suggestions of units to cut that would presumably show our seriousness and save money. In Portland, they say cut Fort Kent and the Colleges of Education or Business at Orono; Downeast, they say cut Lewiston/Auburn; in Lewiston, they target Cooperative Extension; in Brunswick, I'm told to cut football; in Bangor I'm instructed to close

4: Growth and Development of the System

Machias and electrical engineering at USM; among some faculty it's eliminate ITV and among others, it's the Law School; and when I'm not in the room, the most frequent suggestion is to wipe out *my* office. (Woodbury, 1993, p. 3)

It was the best of times and the worst of times during the administrations of John R. McKernan, Jr. The economy of Maine loomed so large that it can be argued that actions by the Governor and the University of Maine System's administrators were reliant, almost to the point of solely dependent, upon it. To underscore the problem faced by state leaders, consider the fact that the University of Maine System's budget request to the State of Maine for fiscal year 1992 was nearly $45 million less than the actual appropriation (Board of Trustees of the University of Maine System, 1990, December 17, p. 3). This request for an increase in the University of Maine System budget had been termed "moderate" by trustee David Flanagan (Board of Trustees of the University of Maine System, 1990, November 12, p. 1).

To point a partisan or philosophical finger of praise or blame under these circumstances can hardly be viewed as rational following an historical analysis of the differing economic climates.

The Term of Chancellor J. Michael Orenduff (1993-1996)

Was the first chancellor ever to receive a vote of no confidence from the System's faculty a poor administrator, a victim of circumstance, or both? It is hard to find opinion in the literature of the day that does not fault Chancellor Orenduff's style of leadership. A suitable examination of the question might be achieved given the passage of time and a full chronicle of the agenda that the Chancellor tried to present.

J. Michael Orenduff can be aptly described as a horse of a different color. He described himself as a "dabbler" and a "dilettante," and has written numerous articles on ethics, logic, and philosophy (Kesseli, 1993, November 16, p. 1). He was a professor of philosophy and department chair at Southwest Texas State before taking the helm as President of the University of Maine at Farmington (UMF) (Kesseli, p. 1). Under Orenduff's leadership, Farmington made vertical cuts during the financial crisis of the early 1990s, eliminating programs such as home economics and continuing education that did not fit in with the

4: Growth and Development of the System

developing campus niche (Kesseli, p. 1). UMF was also the first System campus to abolish its two-year associate-degree program (Kesseli, p. 1). Orenduff was praised as a man of "real vision for the University of Maine at Farmington" by its faculty senate president and as a man of "courage" who was not "afraid to move ahead with things" (Kesseli, p. 1). While Orenduff was at Farmington, *U.S. News and World Report* named the campus among the top 25 percent of liberal arts institutions, and it was also cited as one of the most efficient institutions in a survey by the *Wall Street Journal* (Kesseli, p. 1). By comparison to past system chancellors and according to most published reports, Orenduff became the first Maine chancellor with an established record that reflected a genuine willingness to terminate unworthy or unproductive academic offerings, while at the same time significantly strengthening excellent programs that furthered campus missions.

In a letter from newly appointed Chancellor J. Michael Orenduff to this author, the decision variables in his first year in office were described:

> The trustees have taken seriously the need to respond to the State's financial situation. They have adopted a strategic plan that refines campus missions by sharpening the focus of programs and reducing support costs, while at the same time protecting high quality programs and services. Campus presidents have made--not delayed--difficult decisions: There has been a measurable downsizing. There are 364 fewer employees today than in January 1990 (an 8 percent reduction), and enrollment this fall was 1,165 students below last year. The reduction in staff is in actual full-time regular employees, not in "positions" or "slots" or "vacancies." There are 364 fewer individuals receiving a paycheck from the University now than there were on January 1, 1990. (Orenduff Personal Communication, 1993, December 16)

A chancellor's office can resemble political office in many ways. Many leaders who have made tough decisions or who propose substantive changes have rapidly lost a lot of friends. In the case of Chancellor Orenduff, his vision included program cuts and rapid change, both through the development of institutional downsizing and some

104   *4: Growth and Development of the System*

cutting-edge concepts. The chancellor always seemed to be ahead of the curve, proposing to implement solutions now that might typically be better left for future years. His tenure was also inexorably fused with stalled salary negotiations that left faculty without a raise for several years before he took the post (Hale, 1995, March 14, p. 1).

One of the cutting-edge concepts that had faculty furious was the awarding of degrees through the Educational Network of Maine (EdNet, later called UNET). Although the concept had been around for quite some time, the courses offered over satellite television were viewed by many faculty to be of inferior quality, and there was also serious concern about reuse of tapes. Chancellor Orenduff's original proposal would allow students to be able to earn bachelor's and master's degrees by combining courses from University campuses to be delivered over the network (Young, 1995, January 22, p. 3A). A subsequent proposal was even more progressive. Chancellor Orenduff directed, and the trustees tentatively agreed, to make EdNet a separate eighth campus that would seek accreditation to give it degree-granting authority (Goodman, 1995, March 26, p. 41).

This proposal incensed faculty. They were furious because, on top of their philosophical disagreements, faculty claimed that they had not been consulted (Young, 1995, January 22, p. 3A). Also, the faculty union and others raised questions as to whether administrators were bargaining in good faith about salary. With the specter of salary looming in the background, faculty took to the legislature and the media protesting the EdNet expansion. As one faculty member commented, "Technology is driving this project, rather than educators being able to use the technology as a tool. Education is more than pouring information into student's heads, as if they were sausage casings" (Young, p. 3A). Legislative remedies and media avenues had been explored before, but this time faculty went one step farther by circulating petitions at all seven campuses, calling for a vote of no confidence in Chancellor Orenduff following his annual "State of the University Address" (1995). The issue was befuddled by the several published reports claiming that EdNet would become a program of its own. The Chancellor denied the idea that an eighth campus would exist, stating flatly, "EdNet will not be unilaterally granting degrees" (Young, p. 3A).

Chancellor Orenduff's 1995 "State of the University Address" to the One Hundred and Seventeenth Maine Legislature drew applause on

4: Growth and Development of the System

several occasions, combining a conservative approach emphasizing restructuring and cost efficiency with a progressive batch of new and emerging ideas (Hale, 1995, March 3, p. A1). While legislators and some trustees hailed his ideas, faculty were stunned, as even more changes were advanced by Orenduff without regard to faculty governance and traditional administrative procedures that had been in place in prior administrations. In fact, Orono President Frederick Hutchinson later stepped beyond the bounds of the traditional president/chancellor relationship when he publicly commented that lapses had occurred in the widely accepted practice of "shared governance" (Goodman, 1995, March 26, p. 41).

The Chancellor's support of higher faculty wages in his address sounded hollow in light of the stalled salary negotiations that had dragged on for years, and when he surprised nearly everyone by calling for an exit exam for all students, he crossed into another faculty domain that would not be tolerated. The following comments fanned even more faculty flames, but again won legislators' interest:

> I have been an administrator for a number of years now, and I am convinced that there are too many of us...As we go about restructuring, some people will be displaced....Others will have their pet projects reduced or even eliminated. Those individuals who have a stake in the status quo will feel threatened, as indeed they should be....We need to be straightforward in identifying those activities that have outlived their usefulness and we need to eliminate them. (Hale, 1995, March 3, p. 1A)

Other proposals from Chancellor Orenduff would combine University College in Bangor with the University of Maine at Augusta, offer a single course catalogue for the entire system, and--most disconcerting for faculty--make all courses at all campuses fully transferable (Hale, 1995, March 3, p. 1A). Some legislators may have danced in the hallways when they heard that a chancellor was finally addressing the transfer of credits issue, a constituent problem since 1968. However, the credit-transfer problem had always been a source of contention with faculty concerned over differences between campuses in course content, and reform had been painfully slow to some.

Orenduff did not play the role of guardian of academic integrity very well. With the expectation that course content would always be, by and large, a governance issue that faculty should control, Chancellor Orenduff's comments on transferability stung some faculty.

Although legislative response to Chancellor Orenduff was supportive, it was also guarded. As Representative Mary Small of Bath, a veteran member of the Committee on Education, put it:

> He seems committed to reducing administrative expenses, which is something the legislature has always been interested in... He made valid points about the university being the major job creator... I think there does need to be better dialogue between the trustees and the faculty and the students and the chancellor. (Hale, 1995, March 3, p. A3)

The stress and strain on the System from "The University of Maine Preliminary Downsizing Proposal," which was offered by Orono Campus President Hutchinson in 1993, should also be documented here (Hutchinson, 1993). The tough fiscal times of the early 1990s had taken its toll on the University System, and many faculty and even some administrators felt disenfranchised despite early acceptance of the belt-tightening measures.

Chancellor Orenduff followed this measure by joining trustees in the development of a faculty buyout plan. The buyout allowed the University System to reduce its number of longtime faculty members by 120 (Cheever, 1997, January 1, p. 1). Faculty with at least ten years in the system and who met age requirements were eligible, and more than one third of those participated (Cheever, p. 1). Problems of financing the buyout marred the plan, but it was carried out nevertheless. Having budgeted no money to finance the plan in its first year, future chancellor Terrence MacTaggart and the campus presidents were left with the responsibility of carrying out this proposal. In addition, there was some question as to whether savings could be achieved by the measure.

Similar cost-saving measures were appreciated by cost-conscious observers and were more successful. The Chancellor cut his own office budget and returned one million dollars to assist the state's sagging general fund in 1995 (Hale, 1995, March 3, p. A1). He took heavy

4: Growth and Development of the System

criticism from faculty for the move, but achieved accolades from the executive and legislative branches of government. In November 1997, the Chancellor announced a new program in which the separately constituted Maine Maritime Academy would take advantage of the University System's computer capacity to put their student records and accounting system on-line, saving a substantial amount of money by not having to invest in a system of its own (Board of Trustees of the University of Maine System, 1997, November 10, p. 2).

A nasty scandal in 1994 at the Orono campus over athletic ineligibility also led to a myriad of problems. Allegations of a cover-up of athletic eligibility violations by the athletic director led to a suspension and an investigation by Orenduff (Warner, 1994, April 1, p. 9). His report failed in many ways to reconcile differences between the campus evaluation and conflicting public comments from employees involved in the controversy (Warner, p. 9). The System's relationship with the public was probably at an historic low during this period.

In many ways, Chancellor Orenduff was a man in the wrong place at the wrong time. He confronted problems with new ideas that were of intellectual value, but were probably not very practical. His timing was extremely poor. His miscalculation of the internal environment in the System and his impersonal, top-down approach brought upheaval, brutally undermining his tenure as chancellor. Standoffish trustees who had suffered attacks for years were given a reprieve by way of the blame displacement redirected at Orenduff. The placing of the blame was exemplified by the vote of no confidence by the faculty.

The petition that called for the vote of no confidence was "spearheaded by the Associated Faculties of the University of Maine," the group representing faculty in salary and other labor-relations matters (Hale, 1995, March 14, p. 1). Part of the petition read as follows: "We are taking this action because the Chancellor has arrogantly disregarded the rights, interests, and welfare of faculty and other university workers" (Hale, 1995, March 14, p. 1). The petition went on to say that "He violates due process, refuses to bargain in good faith, and shows an unwillingness to listen to the legitimate concerns of his colleagues" (Hale, p. 1). The petition concluded by highlighting the key failure in the relationship: "We perceive him as an adversary rather than an advocate of the university's mission" (Hale, p. 1).

Faculty senates across the system passed other resolutions that were damaging to Orenduff as well. At Machias, the faculty unanimously endorsed a statement claiming that Orenduff "is undermining the vitality and potential of the university system" and that he "has shown himself to be autocratic and has failed to build consensus for the system's critical role in Maine" (Goodman, 1995, March 26, p. 41). Similarly, the Orono resolution, where nearly half of the University System's faculty are employed, stated that Orenduff "has jeopardized the academic integrity of all the institutions" (Goodman, p. 41).

Trustees were seen backpedaling from Chancellor Orenduff. Trustee Bennett Katz of Augusta, a former legislator, moaned that the "old notion of the academy is really under attack in the minds of many people" (Goodman, March 26, 1995, p. 41).

He later stated, "There are two basic policy questions in education: who pays and whose hands are on the steering wheel. I think the faculty's hands have slipped off the steering wheel" (Goodman, p. 41). Another trustee worried about the impact of the situation on the ability of trustees and administrators to advocate for appropriations in the legislature. "We're going to have trouble....We need to build bridges with the legislature," said Patricia Collins of Caribou to the *Boston Globe* (Goodman, p. 41).

With his campuses "mired in malaise," Orenduff was powerless to battle back (Goodman, 1995, March 26, p. 41). Support even withered in the legislature, with some seriously considering a bill mandating a moratorium on the EdNet issue until another visiting committee could be constituted (Goodman, p. 41).

Chancellor Orenduff resigned in April 1995 despite a Board of Trustees that clumsily decided to announce their support for him just one week earlier. The announcement of support had appeared to only worsen an already impossible situation. Acting Board of Trustee Chairwoman Sally Vamvakias stated that rather than having the System "continue to be compromised by the controversy that has surrounded him in recent weeks," Orenduff had decided to step aside (McCall, 1995, April 3, p. A1). Trustee James Cameron stated the obvious: "The board supported a lot of his ideas, but maybe his style could have been better. I think he realizes that better than anyone. I hope to get this acrimony behind us" (Goodman, 1995, March 26, p. 41).

Robert Woodbury was quickly named Acting Chancellor. By appointing the highly respected former chancellor, some trustees hoped the tense environment would subside. Trustee Vamvakias stated that Woodbury "is in every important respect the ideal person to lead the system during this time of transition and introspection" (Young, 1995, April 6, p. A3). In just five months, Woodbury accomplished the task. Upon acceptance of the position, he exclaimed, "There is no monopoly on wisdom....We've got to have dialogue between the constituencies in the system" (Young, p. A3). It took just one month of that dialogue for Woodbury to relieve pressure. George Connick, who had been appointed President of EdNet, was brought in front of the Board of Trustees and peppered with questions about the program (Young, p. A3). Woodbury admitted that seeking degree-granting authority was premature, stammering, "It does not need to be answered at this time....It may never need to be pursued" (Young, p. A 3).

The Administration of Governor Angus S. King, Jr. (1995-Present)

As the seventy-first Governor of Maine, Angus King appeared to spend a great deal of his time successfully promoting and encouraging business growth. His greatness as governor, as well as his strong popularity, was driven by his support of programs and tax incentives that surely improved both economic performance and the incentives for private interests to invest in Maine. During his first four years in office, many wondered whether Governor King planned to take a role in promoting higher education in the twenty-first century with even a small fraction of the fervor with which he addressed business needs. As a result, much of the information that begins this section highlights activities in the field, major reports, and legislative involvement, rather than actions proposed or endorsed by the Governor.

For example, in the Governor's "Budget in Brief: Summary of the Program and Budget Proposals for Fiscal Years 1996-1997," King said little about his goals for higher education. He did support "growth for the University of Maine System of 1 percent in fiscal year 1996 and 3 percent in fiscal year 1997," but this low percentage increase was based on per annum figures (King, Jr., 1995, p. 38). His 1998 and 1999 budget proposals reflected an even lower funding commitment of 1 and 2 percent, respectively, with the 1999 increase dependent on a "challenge grant" (King, Jr., 1997, p. 40). The proposed spending levels did little to raise the hopes of the higher education community in Maine. Several departments of state experienced budget increases that were much higher during the period, both on a per annum basis and as a percentage of the overall budget. For example, as a percentage of total state budget expenditures, transportation funding approximately doubled from 1994 to 1998, as did funding for public safety (State of Maine, 1999, p. 10). Defense, veterans, emergency management, and economic and community development also received percentage-of-budget increases (State of Maine, 1999, p. 10). When looking at state budget figures, the percentage-of-the-budget method reflects spending priorities in one program as they relate to other programs. Increases in percentage of budget for any major budget component adds up to millions of additional expenditures annually. The higher education component of Governor King's state budget decreased as a percentage of the overall state budget, from 10.67 percent in 1994 to 9.69 percent through the fiscal year ending June 30, 1998 (State of Maine, 1999, p. 10). This added up to an approximate additional expenditure of $14 million for higher education from fiscal years 1994 to 1998, as compared to all other education programs (including primary and secondary education, for example) that experienced an increase in total expenditures of more than $150 million (State of Maine, 1999, p. 10). Legislative wrangling did not increase the numbers for higher education significantly until 1999, when funding for research and development increased. While there are other factors involved, through the fiscal year 2000, funding for higher education continued to be reduced yearly as a percentage of the state budget.

While much of the literature of the time spoke to the successes of the Maine Maritime Academy, the Maine Technical College System, and Maine's private colleges, the University of Maine System experienced a prolonged period of low funding increases, high tuition hikes, and bad press until 1999. This unpleasant combination of events left a mark on the System from which it began to rebound at the end of the century. An examination of the University of Maine System through the middle 1990s revealed several trends. For example, according to the recently completed "Strategic Environmental Assessment of the University of Maine System":

>...Maine ranks very low regarding state support for higher education--nearly always in the bottom five states. Maine ranks

4: *Growth and Development of the System* 111

forty-seventh in the rankings of the Chronicle of Higher Education and forty-ninth by the National Association of State Budget Officers. Indeed, our 4.9 percent level of spending is less than half of the U.S. average of 10.5 percent. (Margaret Chase Smith Center for Public Policy, 1997, p. B2)

As a result of inadequate decision-making and consistent turmoil within the University of Maine System during the middle 1990s, critics began to clamor over insufficiencies in several areas. The Commission on Higher Education Governance was established by the Maine Legislature under Public Law 1995, Chapter 395, to examine the System (P. L. 1995, Chapter 395, Part Q). A special conference was also set up at the University of Maine campus, entitled "Assessing the Environment for Public Higher Education in Maine" (University of Maine, 1995, November 1-2). The complaints about funding and management led to more talk of dismantling the System's structure.

Another report on the University of Maine's future, entitled "The University of Maine System: A Time for Change' (1996), was released to the media by two well-respected former trustees and a Portland lawyer, setting off a flurry of public debate in late 1996 (Carlisle, Wells, & Fitzgerald, November, 1996). The report called for major structural changes, including a system-wide decentralization and elimination of the Chancellor's Office. Another major suggestion made in this report was to move to a voucher system, in which the dollars invested would be assigned to students rather than to the institutions. A loosely followed and even more loosely communicated funding formula had been used in prior years.

In the weeks following this report, former Governor Kenneth Curtis joined in the call for structural change. Governor Curtis called Carlisle's report "extremely thoughtful," stating that the "status quo is probably unacceptable," and that the System had not lived up to "key expectations" (Carrier, 1996, November 17, p. B1). The *Maine Sunday Telegram* editorial board concluded that Curtis should head a commission designed to take a look at changing the overall structure of the University System (Neavoll, 1996, November 24, p. C4). This commission never came to be.

Concerned over reports about the University of Maine System, the Board of Trustees adopted a broad set of positively framed goals in

November 1996, in an effort to counteract the widespread negativism. These goals focused on a theme of "Creating the Positive Agenda" (Board of Trustees of the University of Maine System, 1996, September 30, pp. 1-3). The board appeared to be preparing to fend off a myriad of proposed state legislation, including several bills that echoed the theme of the "Carlisle Report" ("The University of Maine System: A Time for Change") to be referred to as the "Carlisle Report"). During this entire period, Governor King largely stood on the sidelines and observed.

The tone of the debate appeared to change in 1996. Surprisingly, the "Report of the Commission on Higher Education Governance" (1996, July) recommended no structural change, calling for "a truce on the issue" (State of Maine, 1996, July, p. i). The report's conclusions carried more weight with the Maine Legislature than the "Carlisle Report" for many reasons. The most obvious strength of the report was the fact that it was commissioned by the Legislature itself, whereas the "Carlisle Report" was not. In addition, until the most recent recession, many believed that the System had performed admirably. For example, in 1992, in a study conducted in conjunction with the American Association of State Colleges and Universities, Maine's system of public higher education and its leadership were cited as impressive: "When a system board resolves internal problems and disputes by itself--such as allocation of resources--it discourages legislative involvement. This aspect of leadership in Maine impressed us." (Schick, 1992, p. 98). As a result, newly appointed Chancellor Terrence MacTaggart was given a reprieve by the Legislature's Joint Standing Committee on Education. The Committee agreed that the new Chancellor should have at least one year to address concerns.

During this period, enrollment and research issues came to center stage. The new Chancellor's 1997 "Report to the Maine State Legislature" unveiled a plan to boost enrollment by "2000 by the year 2000" (MacTaggart, 1997, p. 3). In addition, David Silvernail, the Director for Educational Policy at the University of Southern Maine, conducted widely read research that took a long, hard look at the prospect of increasing post-secondary enrollments in Maine (Silvernail, 1997, pp. 26-34). In another newspaper report, Andrew Garber explored the continuing competition for enrollments between the flagship Orono campus and the University of Southern Maine, where enrollments had surpassed expectations, climbing to 10,230 full- and part-time students

4: Growth and Development of the System

(Garber, 1997, October 26, p. B16). These individuals and others began to pull the debate back toward enrollment following the unpopular downsizing earlier in the decade. From 1997 to 1999, enrollment climbed by 550 students (Garber, 1999, June 17, p. 1).

On the research front, Dr. George Jacobson, the Director of Quaternary Studies at the University of Maine, issued a report entitled "Higher Education in Maine," and led a group known as the "Faculty Five," which successfully garnered major state appropriations for research and development (Jacobson, Norton, Markowsky, Hunter, & Smith, 1997, p. 1). The "Jumpstart 2000" strategy, as it was termed, was outlined in *The Maine Policy Review* in May 1997 and met surprising success in the state appropriations process (Lawrence and Jacobson, 1997, p. 35). Legislators, aware of Maine's dismal performance in research and development activity in higher education over prior years, were poised to jump at the chance for developments in the field.

This success was furthered by a stark reality. For the most recent year in which data existed, the State of Maine ranked "fiftieth in the United States in per capita spending on university-based research and development" (Lawrence & Jacobson, 1997, p. 35). While the spending on Jumpstart 2000 was far below the original request, the approximately two million dollars offered up for federal matching purposes was achieved with no apparent effort by the executive branch of government. In fact, Governor King did not appear to be involved in the higher education debate to any great degree, leaving the decision with the Maine Legislature. The Legislature did respond. From 1998 to 2000, research and development spending rose from $500,000 to $ 9.5 million (Garber, 1999, July 11, p. 1).

From 1997 to the present, much of the interest from the executive branch regarding higher education keyed on student aspirations. Although development of an aspirations initiative by Maine's system of higher education costs money, it was a low-level investment in comparison to research and development, investment in infrastructure, or other potential new programs. Nevertheless, it was viewed as sound policy in the education arena. Governor King discussed the issue of the aspirations of Maine's youths in many speaking engagements in 1997. The effort to focus on aspirations, however, appeared to have been restarted by faculty, the Board of Trustees, and others. Professor Russell Qualia headed up a newly established aspirations program at the

4: Growth and Development of the System

University of Maine that garnered some attention in 1996, and new Chancellor Terrence MacTaggart strongly endorsed the initiative in his 1997 "State of the University Address," which was aptly entitled "Meeting the Aspirations of Maine People" (MacTaggart, 1997). In the Address, Chancellor MacTaggart outlined a basic starting point for the initiative and emphasized the importance of coupling it with low tuition:

> But, if these students have a strong desire to achieve something high or great, they also fear that an education will be denied them because it costs too much; they are leery of the debt burden of student loans; they are afraid good careers in Maine won't be available for graduates. (MacTaggart, 1997, p. 2)

His aspirations initiative included strengthening the following areas:
1. Stronger ties with K-12
2. A 2000 by the year 2000 enrollment plan
3. A legitimate transfer program
4. University-business partnerships to create jobs (MacTaggart, 1997, pp. 2-4).

His approach was supported by data. In agreeing with many of the previous themes, Silvernail noted that "Maine ranks forty-ninth in student participation in higher education" and that "theories abound" as to why high school seniors have little aspiration to immediately enroll in two- and four-year programs (Silvernail, 1997, pp. 27-28). The September 1997 Board of Trustees meeting announcement on aspirations was highly anticipated. At that meeting, Education Commissioner J. Duke Albanese declared that "student aspirations are at the top of the Governor's list for Maine people because economic growth in the state is dependent on an educated populace" (Board of Trustees of the University of Maine System, 1997, September 22, p. 4). Others publicly joined in to move the aspirations and access initiative forward and to lead debate. Board Chair Sally G. Vamvakias emphasized the role of aspirations in a "knowledge-based economy" (Vamvakias, 1997, p. A17). In his inaugural speech of November 21, 1997, new University of Maine President Peter Hoff sought to clarify the connection between aspirations and access:

Access means making sure that the educational needs of Maine's citizens are met. As a state, we have made progress in raising the educational and professional aspirations of our young people. Where just a decade ago, only 37 percent of our high school graduates went on to college or university, today the number is 46 percent. But some questions remain about where Mainers are getting their college education. While only a decade ago 60 percent of those high school graduates who went on to college did so in Maine, now fewer than half go to college in their home state. In spite of the fact the University of Maine offers an array of academic programs as good and as extensive as any in New England, our entering class this fall represented only about 14 percent of the total Maine high school graduates who went on to college. Those numbers tell me that we are not providing access in a way that works to the State's advantage. (Hoff, 1997, p. 4)

Governor King endorsed the concept of aspirations as defined by higher education administrators in Maine by the middle of 1998. It was not known whether he linked the aspirations initiative with problems like high tuition costs, or whether he intended to recommend substantial increases in state appropriations to lower tuition rates, if indeed the link between aspirations and tuition was made by his administration.

Governor King's contribution to higher education in Maine appeared by many accounts not measurable in any direct terms, unless one factors in the overall economic benefits passed on through the promotion of sustainable job growth. The one major issue that might have defined his administration (in much the same way that the administration of Governor Longley was defined by the medical school veto) was a legislative proposal to offer the first two years of higher education free to all Maine students. It is not known whether Governor King would have supported the expensive concept had the legislature passed L.D. 2213, *An Act to Encourage High School Students to Pursue Higher Education at Post-secondary Institutions in This State*. Most reports had him ready to veto the bill. Supporters claimed that the free tuition proposal went to the heart of the aspirations issue and broke down the most commonly referenced barrier to degree-seekers, that of cost. Opponents viewed the bill as financially unattainable and completely

116   4: Growth and Development of the System

irresponsible. While policymakers, including Governor King himself, continued to try to find ways to encourage Maine citizens to complete post-secondary degrees, one thing was virtually certain: a giant sigh of relief could be heard in the Office of the Governor when the bill was killed in the House of Representatives in the spring of the 1998 gubernatorial election year, never landing on his desk.

Maine's low national rank for residents with completed college degrees has kept the issue of higher education on the front burner. But while the King Administration agreed with the One Hundred Nineteenth Legislature to spend part of the budget surpluses of the late 1990s on public higher education, most of the impetus for this spending came from the legislative branch of Maine government. Nevertheless, the investments that the King Administration made in Maine citizens through steadfast support of economic development incentives like the business equipment tax rebate program almost certainly placed the University System in a stronger long-term financial position, just as the Governor said it would.

The Term of Chancellor Terrence MacTaggart (1996-Present)

The administration of Terrence MacTaggart has been much less turbulent than his predecessor J. Michael Orenduff. Although MacTaggart was thrust into a situation that was far from stable, he was effectively able to stave off major legislative intervention and help quiet the hostilities of faculty and other university constituencies.

Chancellor MacTaggart came from the Minnesota State University System, where he was completing a sabbatical in Thailand as a Fulbright Scholar. According to an Associated Press report from December 1995, he emerged as a top choice when two other candidates withdrew their names from consideration and a third chose not to negotiate (Associated Press, 1995, December 16, p. 5B). MacTaggart was said to be "adept at handling tough issues," and he certainly encountered some from his first day on the job (Cohen, 1995, December 26, p. 1A).

A long recession plagued the State of Maine right up until Chancellor MacTaggart took office, and its effects on the University of Maine System were outlined in detail in the analysis of the McKernan Administration. As MacTaggart took the reigns, some wondered if he understood the weight of the work ahead of him. For example, according to University of Maine Trustee Bennett Katz, budget cuts and the State's

4: Growth and Development of the System

finances were not the only things to be concerned about during the years of retrenchment that characterized the 1990s. Katz made his feelings known to the public, as indicated in the following:

> I suspect that most Maine people who read daily about the State's financial problems shrug their shoulders. Disappointing growth in the State's revenues is not the major problem. It is the conscious political downgrading of the importance of the University as a State priority that is the real tragedy. (Katz, 1995, November 15, p. 6)

The problems faced by the University of Maine System due to issues such as the Katz concern affected the System at all levels. Many students felt that the cuts were shouldered unequally, however. For example, Curtis Marsh, the President of the University College-Bangor Student Senate appeared at a Board of Trustees meeting and spoke of discrimination against students of the University College-Bangor (Board of Trustees of the University of Maine System, 1996, November 18, p. 1). Marsh stated that the University of Maine at Augusta (the parent campus of the University College-Bangor) had been treated unequally over the years by the funding formula used by trustees to disperse the scarce resources made available to the System. As a result, the University College suffered an even heavier hit. Marsh stated that the Student Government Association had retained legal counsel to look into the funding situation and he then gave the Board of Trustees until December 1996 to remedy the situation before official legal action would be taken (Board of Trustees of the University of Maine System, p. 1). The threat never materialized but the point was well taken. Chancellor MacTaggart would be challenged frequently in financing and public relations arenas, but he appeared to respond to each challenge.

Having told trustees that he would limit the use of the University's interactive television component (EdNet), he eased tensions and won early points with the members of the search committee and faculty leaders (Cohen, 1995, December 26, p. 1A). Upon his arrival, he also effectively assessed the remaining backlash from events such as the early-retirement faculty buyout, a plan questioned by some as ineffective. MacTaggart dealt with the faculty buyout with internal management strategies, but he was also required to formulate strategies

4: Growth and Development of the System

based on a hostile external environment in the Maine Legislature. Despite the fact that Acting Chancellor Woodbury had significantly smoothed the rippling waters in just a few months on the job, there were still lingering problems from the Orenduff Administration beyond the buyout plan that needed attention, including the community college conceptual failure, flat funding from the state and poor fund raising efforts, the athletics scandals at Orono, and the academic credit transfer, to name a few.

Chancellor MacTaggart inherited the early retirement/faculty buyout plan from Chancellor Orenduff and some very beleaguered trustees. The buyout allowed the University System to reduce its number of longtime faculty members by 120, but because no money had been budgeted to finance the plan in its first year, Chancellor MacTaggart and campus presidents were left with the responsibility of funding this costly proposal (Cheever, 1997, January 1, p. 1). The faculty bargained to put the benefit in as part of their contract, so MacTaggart and the trustees could do little more than make the best out of an expensive mistake.

Chancellor MacTaggart's real strength was said to be his non-confrontational style in his dealings with the Minnesota Legislature, in areas that ranged from dismissing some presidents to merging community colleges and technical schools with the Minnesota State System (Cohen, 1995, December 26, p. 14A). That strength would be tested during his term due to the publication of three major reports about the University of Maine System. In 1995, a special conference was set up at the University of Maine campus entitled, "Assessing the Environment for Public Higher Education in Maine" (University of Maine, 1995, November 1-2). The one-day conference appeared to be a reaction of sorts to a commission established by the Maine Legislature just prior to MacTaggart's arrival. A reexamination of the structure set up in 1968 was about to begin, and its climax was the consecutive release of three major reports containing troubling news, all within a nine-month period.

Each of the three reports was generated under different circumstances by different constituencies, but they all partially resulted from the controversial tenure of Chancellor Orenduff and partially from flat funding from the State for each of the first six years of the 1990s. Following is an explanation of the three controversial reports.

The three reports were as follows:

4: Growth and Development of the System

(1) July 1996: "The Report of the Commission on Higher Education Governance," Norman Fournier, Chair, and eight others appointed via legislation (State of Maine, 1996). Experts held hearings and took testimony from around the state, and this report was considered the strongest of the three by most onlookers.

(2) November 1996: "The University of Maine System: A Time for Change," by Peter Carlisle, in collaboration with Owen W. Wells and Duane D. Fitzgerald (Carlisle, et al., 1996). Peter Carlisle, a Portland lawyer, published a privately financed report with the help of Wells, a former trustee who had been critical of the System's structure since 1983, and Fitzgerald, a well-known and influential chief operating officer of the Bath Iron Works.

(3) March 1997: "The Strategic Environmental Assessment," presented to Terrence J. MacTaggart, Chancellor, and The Board of Trustees by the Margaret Chase Smith Center for Public Policy of the University of Maine (Margaret Chase Smith Center for Public Policy, 1997). The Board and Chancellor authorized this report in response to prevailing circumstances, but surprising results were contained in this document, which focused on the perceptions of students and institutional best-practices research. The report was not contentious, probably as a result of the fact that it was not widely distributed, especially among faculty.

The Commission on Higher Education Governance was formed to look into the perceived problems of the University of Maine System. The "Report of the Commission on Higher Education Governance" opened with a sharp statement:

...what the Commission has found is a remarkable disconnect between the public, the government, and the institutions of higher education. In the past, such disconnect may have been attributed to a misunderstanding or misinformation, but this time it's different. The disconnect seems to have become synonymous with distrust. Parents and students can't understand why tuition has soared at twice the rate of inflation, elected officials search furiously for greater accountability for the public dollar, and higher education watches in disbelief as it struggles along with flat funding and a shrinking percentage of the State budget. Buildings deteriorate, enrollments remain flat, and the most precious commodity of all in higher education--an institution's reputation--hangs in the balance. (State of Maine, 1996, p. i)

The data reviewed by the Commission during its efforts documented the weakened environment surrounding Maine higher education and was cause for concern for everybody, not just MacTaggart. The combination of current controversies and a poor showing during the investigation process alerted leaders in politics and in higher education that all was not well. According to census data from 1990, Maine was far ahead of the national average and other New England states in the percentage of students completing high school. Yet in the same 1990 census, Maine lagged behind other states in the percentages of residents completing a bachelor's degree and a graduate degree (State of Maine, 1996). Chancellors from McNeil to MacTaggart had noted that the low number of Maine residents with baccalaureate degrees was a major problem for the State. This phenomenon continued through the end of the century, and there was uncertainty among onlookers as to the cause for it.

Other data reviewed by the Commission complicated matters further by pointing out that despite the low rates of student success in Maine, the State's spending on higher education did not keep pace with other priorities from 1989 through 1996. The University System fared poorly, with a cumulative percent change in appropriations for those years of negative 1.8 percent. Certainly the long, lingering recession that characterized the State of Maine in the early and mid-1990s played a large role in the reduction of support levels from State coffers. Flat funding by the State for seven straight years put the entire System in a precarious position. In the budget year following the report, funding increased by less than 2 percent. These lean years have had system-wide impacts. For example, the average faculty salary of $44,290 in the 1995/1996 academic year did not compare favorably with other states and is probably a deterrent to good faculty recruitment (State of Maine, 1996, Appendix Five).

Testimony and fact-finding was extensive, lending credibility to the report. The procedure was typical for a government task force, but

4: Growth and Development of the System 121

involved far more public input, key testimony, and recommendations. The model of communications flows are outlined in Figure 4.1 through the following author's schematic:

Flowchart of Communications, Commission on Higher Education Governance:

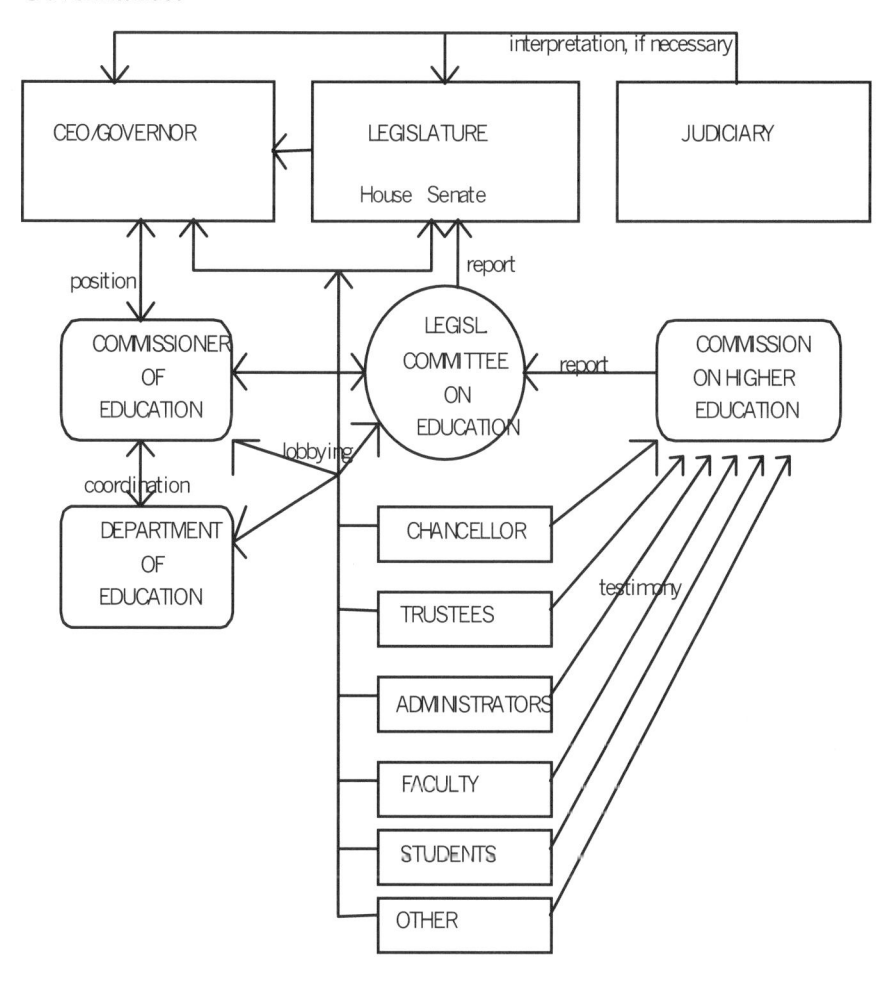

Figure 4.1: Communication Flows, Commission on Higher Education Governance

This report involved more input and was better communicated than any other report since the Visiting Committee's work in 1986. Chancellor MacTaggart, the new kid on the block, inherited the Commission's report. The report was critical of the System as a whole, but stopped short of attacking its structure as a cause for what was generally perceived as the crisis years from 1995 to the middle of 1997.

The Commission was confronted with an environment in Maine that caused trustees to turn to tuition increases often. Maine residents' low median family income and other factors made tuition increases of the magnitude of the 1990s a difficult barrier for them to overcome. Groups around the state targeted the affordability of higher education in Maine as one of the top reasons why so many of Maine's high school graduates did not consider college. The future could lead to an even lower expectation for educational excellence in Maine, because in addition to the low levels of baccalaureate degree attainment, the community college system was not functioning well.

The clamor for change appeared to reach its peak with the issuance of another report in 1996 (mentioned previously) entitled, "The University of Maine System: A Time for Change" (Carlisle, et al., 1996). This document was impressively researched and written by a group of former alumni and trustees of the system, and as such it received notable publicity. Just a few months following the Commission on Higher Education's report, Carlisle, Wells, and Fitzgerald smartly timed the release of their report. In a major surprise, former Governor Curtis publicly approved of the approach. With Curtis critical of the performance of the System, trustees seemed to scramble for answers in 1997 and 1998. Major legislation was introduced in the Maine Legislature that mirrored the recommendations from the report.

The third major report compiled at this time was "The Strategic Environmental Assessment" (Margaret Chase Smith Center, 1997). The assessment may have been a simple attempt by trustees to learn more about the higher education environment. Alternatively, it may have been perceived as Chancellor MacTaggart's attempt at offsetting the other two reports. If so, the results caused that strategy to misfire.

A comparison of the three reports exposed contradictions between them. "The Strategic Environmental Assessment" was one of the few reports that focused heavily on student perceptions in addition to compilation of the usual sources of secondary research. In addition to

4: Growth and Development of the System 123

demographic, economic, fiscal data, and best practices research, major primary data was collected through a scientific telephone survey of 524 University of Maine System students and five statewide focus groups (Margaret Chase Smith Center, p. 2). Although not conducted on a yearly basis, the telephone survey has been completed three times in the 1990s. Qualitative focus group data was finally compiled and examined after what appeared to be years of ignorance of the importance of this type of research in Maine.

Of the three reports, "The Strategic Environmental Assessment" best attempted to address concerns raised by students. The questionnaire and focus-group data gathered by the Margaret Chase Smith Center (University of Maine) and the Muskie Institute (University of Southern Maine) caused report recommendations to be geared toward student concerns. What exactly were these concerns and how do they relate to the rest of the debate?

The "Strategic Environmental Assessment's" questionnaire data was confined to the university experience. The general focus was on current practices. Nevertheless, it appeared that understanding the current environment on each campus went a long way toward a better grasp of the System's many problems.

Focus-group responses were far more useful and revealing than the questionnaire, particularly regarding the image of the system. Three themes were recurrent throughout the focus groups:

- a concern for the lack of consensus regarding the responsibilities and priorities of the University of Maine System;
- the belief that the System was not meeting current responsibilities in a satisfactory manner; and
- a concern that the System had not satisfactorily communicated its contributions to Maine leaders (Margaret Chase Smith Center, 1997, p. 10-11).

The focus groups spent more time on the future needs of the System and its overall direction. Five future priorities were delineated and were widely shared across the focus groups. According to the report, the System should:

- set standards for educational quality and accessibility for the campuses, as well as for higher education in the state;
- better understand, represent, and communicate with critical constituencies;
- foster open and continuing dialogue about the System and higher education issues in the state;
- do a better job of teaching "twenty-first century skills," such as understanding technological systems and thinking critically; and
- guarantee and deliver Maine citizens affordable and accessible opportunities for higher education (Margaret Chase Smith Center, 1997, p. 11).

Because focus groups and the system-wide questionnaire were both utilized, the "Strategic Environmental Assessment" developed eight integrated recommendations that were clearly more representative of student needs, with the best example being the focus on tuition. "The Carlisle Report" and "The Report of the Commission on Higher Education Governance" appeared to be more representative of other non-student interest groups that had a stake in the process. A synopsis of the final recommendations of the University of Maine System's "Strategic Environmental Assessment" indicated that the University of Maine needed improvement in the following areas:

1. Responding to Demographic and Economic Trends: including developing more programs linked to the state economy, communicating the return on university investment, and aggressive recruiting techniques

2. Clearly Communicating a Vision and Mission: including solicitation of critics' views and emphasizing the role of the Chancellor

3. Better Performance Measurement and Systematic Analysis: through development of a better performance measurement mechanism and benchmarking and a systematic collection of qualitative and quantitative data

4. Improve Structure and Inter-System Relationships: including debate of the tenure system's usefulness and clarification of relationships between interfacing institutions

4: Growth and Development of the System

5. Promote Change as a Participatory Process: through recommitting the System to a process of shared governance, clear lines of communication, and bringing an end to the failed downswing policies of the past

6. Reinvigorating the Undergraduate Curriculum: placing a priority on assistance from employers but making a clear distinction between job-specific training and other modes of higher education; exploring a curricula reward system emphasizing interdisciplinary approaches, lifelong learning, and analytical abilities

7. Reassessment of the Graduate Curriculum: including an affirmation of community leadership roles and a demand assessment of degree offerings

8. Recognition of a Broad Array of Delivery Modes: including aggressive pursuit of distance education through computer and interactive television

9. Improved Support for Research and Public Service Initiatives: encouraging emphasis on Maine community research and dramatically elevating the importance of research and development in improving Maine's quality of life and economic capacity (for more detailed recommendations, see Margaret Chase Smith Center, 1997, pp. 17-22).

As opposed to "The Strategic Environmental Assessment," "The Carlisle Report" had the feel of an outsider looking in, and for just cause. Despite the fact that the authors were well respected and had long-held ties to the University of Maine System, the vast changes proposed were viewed by some as radical. The idea of a voucher system had ramifications that struck chords across political spectrums. Legislation based on the report failed miserably in the Maine Legislature, but some suggestions made within it were favored. Good research of university operations in other states combined with a business-oriented, competitiveness-based approach strengthened its merits. As the "Carlisle Report" stated:

> States with central governance systems are not accountable to the students; rather, they look to the state legislatures for their

appropriations and to the federal government and outside funding sources for research grants. Since faculty reputations are built upon research, not teaching, and since grants bring money, research is and has been elevated in priority to the detriment of teaching. In most centralized systems, the bottom line has become so vague as to be indistinguishable. Since the system itself is protected from the market forces, the system creates expensive layers of administration and bureaucracy to fabricate and maintain a system of artificial forces--designed to simulate the actual economic and competitive forces--in an attempt to foster and gauge some level of quality and efficiency. Subjecting higher education to the actual market forces eliminates many of the bureaucratic costs and gives birth to a variety of entrepreneurial movements. (Carlisle, 1996, p. 17)

Many Maine people began to recognize problems associated with a central governance system, and statewide discussion was elevated by the market-oriented approach espoused in the report.

As was outlined earlier, "The Commission on Higher Education Governance Report (C.H.E.G.)" took a different approach, defending the current governance structure of the University of Maine System. The report focused more heavily on the amount of dollars invested (Carrier, November 17, 1996, p. B1). For example, the first five recommendations featured large dollar investments "in Maine's future economic well-being" (State of Maine, 1996, pp. 13-14). These recommendations included development of a method of predictable funding that would include mandated cost-of-living adjustments, a doubling of access to technical education, an increase in infrastructure allocations, major new investments in research and development, and a five-year commitment to allocation increases in the Maine Student Incentive Scholarship Program. Remaining recommendations apparently sought to make political statements about the System structure, trustees, mission, endowment, and the Education Network of Maine. The recommendation for the Education Network of Maine not to have degree-granting authority catered to comments by some faculty fearful of diminishing the value of the campus-based approach, but seemed to run counter to trends in other states. Institutions such as Walden University in Minneapolis, Minnesota, and many others had already begun to offer fully accredited

4: Growth and Development of the System 127

master's degree programs over the Internet, and the trend was growing even stronger by the end of the century. In Maine, for example, several colleges appeared ready to offer a multitude of online degrees in response to the slowly developing approach to online degrees at the University of Maine. The University's heavy investment in the technical equipment required to operate the Educational Network of Maine's audio, video, and online service makes completely online degrees feasible. The end of the century began to make Chancellor Orenduff's original vision to grant online degrees through the Network look like the work of a genius.

Taken together, these three reports contained several serious differences, as well as some key similarities. It can be safely concluded that all three reports note that the image of the System was damaged. The "C.H.E.G. Report" blamed the image problem on the Legislature after flat funding the system for seven consecutive years. "The Carlisle Report" blamed faulty funding mechanisms such as the current allocation formula between campuses, along with the centralization of the structure. "The Strategic Environmental Assessment" was more student-based in its findings, clearly blaming the image issue on the athletic department, leadership, communications, and public relations. Student focus-group participants spent a great deal of time discussing problems of campus administration and lack of communication between the Board of Trustees and those who had a stake in the University System. Other major comparative elements included the following:

1. A vast difference in the view of distance education. "The Strategic Environmental Assessment" chose to promote an all-systems-go approach, as opposed to the "C.H.E.G. Report's" condemnation of the Education Network of Maine as a full-fledged, degree-granting institution. Although "The C.H.E.G. Report" praised the network as a learning tool with great potential, the Commission was "unequivocal in its belief that the network is a service of the university system and as such does not qualify as a campus, nor should it be considered as such" (State of Maine, 1996, p. 27).

2. "The C.H.E.G. Report" and "The Strategic Environmental Assessment" recommend solutions within the current structural

framework. "The Carlisle Report" did not, offering decentralization and restructuring as the preferred alternative.

3. "The C.H.E.G. Report" and "The Strategic Environmental Assessment" looked to increase state funding and improve public relations. "The Carlisle Report" assumed that this could not be achieved without major change in financial relationships.

4. All reports stressed the importance of research and development, although "The Carlisle Report" was critical of research at the sacrifice of good teaching. The clear emphasis on this topic may well have been the impetus for Maine's substantial investment in research and development in 1999.

5. "The Strategic Environmental Assessment" called for linking more academic programs with the State's economy. "The Carlisle Report" believed that this link would develop within a more competitive, decentralized campus framework.

6. "The Carlisle Report" and "The Strategic Environmental Assessment" advocated a best practices review and approach. The "C.H.E.G. Report" believed that performance budgeting, cost-sharing, and privatization held the key to new best practices.

A surprise leader of the higher education debate in 1996 was retired Governor Curtis, the System's founding governor. Curtis reviewed the state of the University of Maine System for the *Maine Sunday Telegram* in an article entitled, "Curtis Joins Critics of the University System" (Carrier, 1996, November 17, p. 12B). With the advantage of having been one of its founders, Governor Curtis understood its faults. Curtis noted that the System had not made it easy to transfer credits, and that not enough had been done to eliminate duplication of courses and degree offerings between campuses (Carrier, p. 12B). In addition, he believed that the centralization of administrative services was no longer necessary (Carrier, p. 12B). Curtis endorsed "The Carlisle Report" that would revamp and decentralize the System's governance structure, and he stood squarely behind a voucher system for Maine students (Carrier, p. 12B). His reentry into the debate on higher education prompted more calls for

4: Growth and Development of the System

study commissions to go beyond the work of the Commission on Higher Education Governance. As former Senate President Jeffrey Butland predicted, however, the new chancellor would intervene. Butland predicted that Chancellor MacTaggart would persuade undecided lawmakers that he had not been on the job long enough to "work his magic" (Carrier, p. 12B).

Senator Butland turned out to be correct. The University of Maine System Board of Trustees adopted the broad set of positively framed goals in November 1996 focusing on the theme of "Creating the Positive Agenda" (Board of Trustees of the University of Maine System, September 30, 1996, pp. 1-3). The Board and Chancellor MacTaggart went into high gear to successfully fend off the myriad of legislative reform proposals including bills that echoed the theme of "The Carlisle Report."

MacTaggart proved to have the experience and personal traits to succeed in the difficult environment. A myriad of legislative programs designed to restructure the University of Maine System were effectively stymied by MacTaggart and key trustees in the hearing room of the Maine Legislature's Joint Standing Committee on Education and Cultural Affairs. For example, a *Bangor Daily News* column entitled "Plethora of Bills Set to Overhaul UMaine System" described legislative attempts to eliminate the chancellor's office, create voucher systems, and allow campuses to have their own boards (Young, 1997, February 1, pp. A1, A8). Many of these bills were based on the Wells-Fitzgerald-Carlisle report. But in the end, the only bill that survived was a measure that created a board of visitors for each campus, reviewed the current funding formula that divides appropriations by campus, and more clearly defined the roles of the chancellor and trustees (Young, 1997, July 12, p. B1).

MacTaggart got much of the credit for the new law's closer proximity to the views of trustees and University supporters (Young, 1997, July 12, p. B8). His newness to the role of chancellor bought him critical time among legislators who were tiring of the failures of the University System to address policy problems with long histories, such as the transferability of credits issue (Young, p. B8)

In the meantime, trustees adopted new goals that were more to the public's liking, including substantive approaches to improve communications with trustees, ensuring cost efficiencies, and strengthening ties with public schools (Board of Trustees of the

University of Maine System, 1996, September 30, pp. 1-2). The Board of Visitors concept was a scheme already in the works and was completed for each campus by 1999. Board of Visitors at each of the campuses could assist in raising money and identifying new programs. By appointing strong local leaders to visiting boards, there was a prevailing opinion even among critics of the University System structure that the direction was a positive one. For example, Owen Wells, a longtime proponent of restructuring the University of Maine System into autonomous campuses, bought into the concept. "Things are moving in the right direction and I'm pleased about that," said Wells (Young, 1997, July 12, p. B8).

Chancellor MacTaggart went on to advocate for the University of Maine System as expected. He approached Governor King with an appropriations request that would raise state spending by $3 million (Perry, 1996, September 29, pp. 1A and 8A). Unfortunately for the Chancellor, the Governor was not willing to buy into the request. King believed that if the University wanted to create new programs or increase scholarships, it needed to look at other programs to be cut to pay for it (Perry, 1996, September 29, p. 8A). Senate President Jeffrey Butland commented further that legislators should take a fresh look at whether the University had too many campuses and satellite schools (Perry, 1996, p. 8A).

One problem that MacTaggart couldn't solve was the perceived high level of tuition. From 1989 to 1996, the rate of tuition had doubled, while at the same time, the System had endured what amounted to a freeze in state appropriations (Perry, 1996, September 29, p. 8A). In fact, state spending on the University of Maine System (not in constant dollars) amounted to $137 million in 1990, and totaled only $135 million in 1997 (Perry, p. 8A). Some legislators stated that the University was still a good investment, and others expressed "a sense out there among people that the university gets enough money already" (Perry, p. 8A). According to Chancellor MacTaggart, the average graduating student had "a diploma in one hand and a $13,000 IOU in the other" (Perry, p. 8A). For many students, the IOU compared well with private school tuition, but for others, there was great hesitation. The tuition debate of 1996 was clouded by a report that fifty-eight of eighty-eight top Maine scholars turned down offers of free tuition from a scholarship program that had been run over the course of eleven years by the Maine Education

4: Growth and Development of the System

Association (Perry, 1996, December 8, p. 1B). Maine's level of tuition for public universities has been high in national comparisons, but was the lowest in New England in 1996 (Perry, 1996, September 29, p. 8A).

Chancellor MacTaggart's 1997 "Report to the Maine State Legislature" brought forth the plan to boost enrollment by 2,000 by the year 2000 (MacTaggart, 1997, p. 3). Interestingly, this plan was a complete reversal from the decade of downsizing strategy employed at some campuses in the System. As a result of the inclusion of enrollment in the discussion (particularly at the land-grant institution in Orono), new strategy was devised to increase the number of students in the Maine System. In Orono, an action plan entitled "BearWorks" was drafted by recently installed President Peter Hoff (Hoff, 1998, February 23). This document outlined an enrollment plan to "rebound to a campus population of 12,000 undergraduate and graduate students and establish a reasonable but aggressive timetable" (Hoff, p. 5). One of the methods to be employed to accomplish this goal was an aggressive recruitment of out-of-state students, "where they may reach an enrollment of as much as 25 percent of the total student population" (Hoff, p. 5). In an interview conducted by the *Maine Times* in August 1998, Hoff explains:

> ...now that we have our act together in addressing in-state needs, I think we're going to look out of state to maybe diversify the student body, bring in different kinds of people with different interests, and serve a wider area. But our first duty is always to serve the students of Maine. (Skelton, 1998, p. 4)

With the Board of Trustees blessing, the new strategy was set for the 1999-2000 academic year.

This strategy also reflected Chancellor MacTaggart's managerial style and belief that campus presidents should play a larger role in directing the future of their campuses. In his nationally acclaimed book *Seeking Excellence Through Independence*, MacTaggart details his goals for Maine:

> Coordinating and governing boards need to work with campus and state leaders in reimagining their roles in a world that demands greater autonomy at the local level, while

4: Growth and Development of the System

simultaneously expecting more focused and efficient service from higher education collectively. The 'entrepreneurial university-efficient system' model being implemented in Maine illustrates one attempt to reconfigure the partnership among the campus, board, and the state. Maine's public university trustees recognized that state support would continue to be low for the foreseeable future, that the state suffers a dearth of baccalaureate degree holders compared to other New England states, and that it possesses a diverse system. Components include a land-grant university, a growing urban institution, a public liberal arts college, regional campuses in rural areas, and a nontraditional institution with substantial distance education programs. With all this in mind, trustees embarked on a consistent effort to reengineer its management and governance practices.

...The result has been a devolution of some authority to campus presidents for decisions over tuition rates, faculty salaries, and admissions policies, along with higher expectations for private fundraising. The System office now plays a stronger role in public and legislative advocacy, managing technology, and setting priorities for funding....The legislature created strong local advisory boards in 1997 to democratize decision-making further, while it affirmed the authority and responsibility of the trustees and the system chancellor. The intent of these changes has been to enable campus presidents to exercise greater freedom while holding them responsible for addressing prominent regional and state needs, notably economic development. The system and the board have accepted the challenge of demonstrating that a system that is simultaneously decentralized and focused on state priorities offers a better alternative than either no-holds-barred competition or authoritarian control. (MacTaggart, 1998, pp. 187-188)

MacTaggart's ideal governance system combined a tractable approach to governors and legislatures with a pass-the-torch-to-the-presidents attitude on campus. If campus presidents were willing to implement idealistic governance mechanisms such as the principles of shared governance, the possibility of campus tranquility not seen in Maine since the late 1980s could be achieved.

4: Growth and Development of the System

Chancellor MacTaggart's guidance of the University of Maine System had received high marks as of the new century, especially in regard to his handling complex governance issues that were exacerbated by three very different reports. It is safe to say that for the two-year period prior to entering the new century, public higher education in Maine was being left to its board and administrators to govern without its political leaders second-guessing its actions.

Before moving to the analysis and results section of this book, it should be noted that the portraits of chancellors and governors that presided over the University of Maine System are in Appendix C.

CHAPTER FIVE: ANALYSIS

> *This research showed that the University of Maine System's ability to adjust to political interventions preserved its viability as a unified mechanism.*

Principles of Analysis

How well does the University of Maine System function? Three principles identified by Yin served as a foundation for this content analysis:

(1) The inquiry dealt with a technically distinctive situation; in this case, the exploration of political interventions upon a single state's governance structure for higher education. The study was buttressed by background information on other familiar governance structures located in other states.

(2) The inquiry relied on the convergence of multiple sources of data. For this case, those sources were documented in Table 3.1 of this document.

(3) The inquiry benefited from the application of a widely held theoretical proposition; namely, that there have been increasing levels of government intervention upon the governance of higher education in the United States (Yin, 1994, p. 13).

This book sought to accomplish three major functions. One result of the analysis was the compilation of a detailed history of the actions and behaviors of the University of Maine System since 1968. These events have been archived in Chapter 4. The thirty-two-year historical and political account is the first ever compiled on the University of Maine System as a whole.

Chapter 5 offers a second component of the research project, using the principles of content analysis and a case-study methodology formatted in a distinct, factual manner. A step-by-step exploration of historically documented events, defined specifically as major political interventions, was undertaken for the purpose of identifying circumstances that exhibit characteristics related to political interventions into the established policies of a unified system. Resulting behavior is then analyzed in the context of the unified structural design of the University of Maine System. This section can be considered new research, in that there has been very little documentation of the pliancy and resiliency of governance systems for higher education as they interrelate with external pressures from forces such as state governments. The best national research to date emanates from the California Higher Education Policy Center.

The third part of the analysis is an exercise matching the historical behavior of the University of Maine System with its original goals. Will the critics' claims of unaccountable boards withstand a detailed historical accounting of board actions? Results of this analysis appear later in the chapter.

The Political Interventions Model

This chapter first documents the result of each intervention in terms of policy actions, as demonstrated as follows:

Intervener → Political Intervention (event) → Policy Action (response/result)

Figure 5.1: Model of Political Intervention Analysis

The exploratory model highlighted in this chapter provided the most important findings of this study. Movements of a unified system of higher education governance were tracked at the very moments that the University of Maine System was being bombarded by outside stimuli; namely, forceful and not-so-forceful political pressures to behave in a way that is different from policy statements and positions of the System's Board of Trustees. As will be seen, this is the part of the study that came to demonstrate pliancy to these interventions and in the long run, system endurance. Readers familiar with other states may draw their own conclusions about whether Maine's unified system compares well or poorly with other systems. Observations about flexibility and

5: *Analysis* 137

resiliency are made in this chapter within the context of this single-state format.

The following assumptions were made in this exercise:

(a) That state government intervention into university governance is inevitable, particularly in a public system of higher education.

(b) That governance structures provide differing levels of guardianship over a system. For example, structures cosseted by state constitutions, particularly those protected by supermajority votes of the legislature, offer different levels of protection from political interventions into a system than those that are statutorily created. Under this hypothesis, direct comparison of systems with vastly different structures become increasingly complex.

(c) That the content analysis method is a preferable method of inquiry for this type of policy problem, in that it has the potential to yield policy options for practitioners involved in the management of higher education. Users of this information may include administrators at the state planning/agency level, state legislators or governors, and may also include university faculty, administrators, presidents, trustees, chancellors, and others.

In this part of the study, the theory that was tested was retrofitted to the State of Maine for the purposes of baseline identification of the issues. This theory appears within the context of the following proposition:

That unified agency structures, designed by law for the delivery of a multi-campus system of higher education, are measurably responsive to increasing levels of government intervention.

The level of responsiveness will then be evaluated. The documented actions are tested based on the previous proposition and are identified by the frequency of their appearance in testimony, editorials, news articles, speeches, campaign rhetoric, minutes, and many other sources described in Table 3.1. Only those issues that clearly meet the definition of an attempted political intervention are evaluated, regardless of whether or

138   5: Analysis

not these interventions caused a major change to come about. The object of this exercise will not be to prove whether political interventions are positive or negative events; rather, the goal is to describe interventions and evaluate their impact. Each part of this exercise is described as follows:
Part 1: Defining an Attempted Political Intervention
Part 2: Identification of the Issues of Political Significance
Part 3: Identification of the Responsible Entity
Part 4: Identification of the Action Resulting from the Political Intervention
Part 5: Findings

Each phase relies on its antecedent until a case is assembled in building-block fashion, with the support of the historical analysis conducted thus far.

Part 1: Defining Attempted Political Intervention
To develop a model to evaluate material, it was necessary to define the term "attempted political intervention." For the purposes of this study, a description of political intervention was sought, but national research failed to yield a suitable definition. Part of the problem with the national literature had to do with preconceptions about the value of political interventions. A good example is Hines' excellent research entitled "Higher Education and State Governments." Hines' research, done on behalf of the Association for the Study of Higher Education, was a groundbreaking effort built on many previous works. Nevertheless, despite Hines' recognition of some of the important aspects of political partnerships, he chose instead to treat interventions with a negative connotation by calling them "intrusions" in all cases (Hines, 1988, pp. 38-39). Hines' description and explanation follows:

> Inappropriate political intrusion occurs when someone in government intercedes in decision-making because of political interest... The appropriate role for the state in higher education is to protect the public's interest through mechanisms for accountability and to create a climate where institutions of higher education thrive. (Hines, 1988, p. 39)

5: Analysis

This description of the interplay between the state and higher education can be found in research documents from before Hines' time to the present. Part of the problem with this approach is the lack of recognition of the original intent of an individual state's structural design. Thoughtful researchers are now recognizing that some structures purposefully allow for specific levels of state government involvement. Recent studies have identified this contextual nature of political involvement and have avoided such blanket treatments (see Bowen, Bracco, Callan, Finney, Richardson & Trombley, 1997, and MacTaggart, 1998). The success or failure of a political intervention may greatly depend on individual nuances between state structures that may invite, allow, or rebuff certain types of interface between state government and public higher education. The real challenge facing field researchers is to find an optimal balance for state government based on predefined criteria acceptable to an amalgamation of interested onlookers.

As a result of the previous analysis, a new and original definition for attempted political intervention was developed for use in this research, as follows:

> An attempted political intervention is an action of political purpose taken by an elected official, interest group, or entity operating outside the sphere of legally delegated authority over higher education that aspires to change previously defined policy statements created by the higher education authority.

Actions of political purpose are attempted daily. Because of this fact, one weakness of this analysis is that it ignored interventions of a lesser scale. In the interest of maintaining content validity, it was decided that emphasis would be placed on events widely considered as major policy issues relating to the Maine System. High levels of controversy characterized these issues. In addition, each event had system-wide implications. In effect, public outcry and controversy were enabling elements for the model.

With Part One now completed, we move to Part Two of the analysis.

Part 2: Identification of the Issues

The history of the institution that is the University of Maine System has been well documented in previous chapters. Based on all that was discovered from investigating the System's history, the following events fit the model of analysis used in this research:

Issues of Political Significance to the University System

Date	Event
1969	First bond issue, $22 million capital improvement
1973	Governor's Blue Ribbon cost-management survey
1974	Governor Longley threatens to fire chancellor
1975	Longley veto of medical school
1975	Longley asks entire Board of Trustees to step down
1976	Governor demands that out-of-state student tuition is raised
1982	Editorial writers/public/legislators join student demands for divestiture of South African holdings
1983	Salary and tenure flap over proposal for Chancellor to resign to become full professor
1986	Report of the Visiting Committee to the University of Maine
1986	Jack Freeman's salary and housing allowance criticized by legislators
1986	Interactive television and library network bond issue
1995	Educational network campus proposal
1996/1997	Three major reports for reform

Table 5.1: Issues of Political Significance to the University System

Each issue/event was described in Chapter 4. Now that these issues have been compiled, they will be assigned appropriate entities most responsible for their occurrence in Part Three.

Part 3: Identification of Responsible Intervener

In the middle column below, the entity(s) most responsible for a major political intervention is identified.

Identification of Political Interveners

Date	Responsible Political Intervener	Event
1969	Voters	First bond issue, $22 million capital improvement
1973	Governor Curtis and Longley	Governor's Blue Ribbon cost-management survey
1974	Governor Longley	Governor Longley threatens to fire chancellor
1975	Governor Longley	Longley veto of medical school
1975	Governor Longley	Longley asks entire Board of Trustees to step down
1976	Governor Longley	Governor demands that out-of-state student tuition is raised
1982	Media/Students	Editorial writers/public/legislators join student demands for divestiture of South African holdings
1983	Legislators/ Faculty	Salary and tenure flap over proposal for Chancellor to resign to become full professor
1986	Governor Brennan	Report of the Visiting Committee to the University of Maine
1986	Senator Baldacci	Jack Freeman's salary and housing allowance criticized by legislators
1986	Voters	Interactive television and library network bond issue
1995	Legislators/ Faculty	Educational network campus proposal
1996/ 1997	Private Citizens	Three major reports for reform

Table 5. 2: Identification of Political Interveners

By previously identifying the issues (Part One), an investigation of historical events then led to the identification of responsible political interveners. In the following grid (Table 5.3), the substantive action resulting from the political intervention is identified.

Part 4: Results

The last column to the right identifies the result of each forceful intervention.

Results of Forceful Political Interventions

Date	Responsible Political Intervener	Event	Substantive Action
1969	Voters	First bond issue, $22 million capital improvement	Defeated
1973	Governor Curtis and James Longley	Governor's Blue Ribbon cost-management survey	Major Revisions Ignored by Trustees
1974	Governor Longley	Governor Longley threatens to fire chancellor	Chancellor Resigns
1975	Governor Longley	Longley veto of medical school	Medical School Dropped
1975	Governor Longley	Longley asks entire Board of Trustees to step down	Governor Ignored
1976	Governor Longley	Governor demands that out-of-state student tuition be raised	Trustees Drop Prior proposal
1982	Media/ Students	Editorial writers/ public/ legislators join student demands for divestiture of South African holdings	Trustees Divest
1983	Legislators/ Faculty	Salary and tenure flap over proposal for Chancellor McCarthy to resign to become full professor	Resignation Not Accepted by Trustees
1986	Governor Brennan	Report of the Visiting Committee to the University of Maine	Report Endorsed by Trustees

1986	Senator Baldacci	Jack Freeman's salary and housing allowance criticized by legislators	Freeman Resigns After 2 Weeks
1986	Voters	Interactive television and library network bond issue	Passed and Implemented
1995	Legislators/ Faculty	Educational network campus proposal	Trustees and Chancellor Reconsider
1996/ 1997	Private Citizens	Three major reports for reform	Trustees Install Visiting Boards in 1998

Table 5.3: Results of Forceful Political Interventions

Part 5: Findings

No responsible practitioner or researcher wants to assemble a better understanding of the governance mechanism in order that the University build higher walls between itself and the rest of the world, or so that the State can micromanage its university system at will. Better knowledge in this area should be developed and used constructively. Newman's words of wisdom from the classic case, *Choosing Quality* (1987), remind us of a noble approach: "By far the most important ingredient of a successful effort to build a university of high quality is a common aspiration to that end" (Newman, 1987, p. 89).

How does Maine's unified system of governance allow it to respond to political intervention? This question is a most important one, not just in Maine, but nationally. Understanding the effectiveness of a prefabricated interfacing mechanism in a university system's structure might in turn yield a better understanding of how to develop a stronger relationship between the university and the state. Systemic adjustments would be less apt to yield haphazard results under such conditions. A better handle on this mechanism might go as far as to assist policymakers in determining exactly which policy proposals to advocate under certain conditions, as well as determining the best method of advocacy.

For example, how does the board best handle the necessary political interface under conditions that include a governor who is hostile to the proposals of public higher education? In the case of Governor James B. Longley's tenure over higher education, examples abound. When

Governor Longley asked trustees to step down, he did so in a joint convention of the Maine Legislature (Palm, 1975, p. 36). Trustee Jean Sampson knew that the board was within its legal authority to say no, and she pointed that out to the media and legislators following the joint convention (Palm, 1975, p. 36). Several legislators sensed that Governor Longley lacked the authority to make the demand, and they rallied to the defense of the structure. Representative David Bustin of Augusta called Longley's demand "an attempt to circumvent the checks and balances built into the university system" (Palm, 1975, p. 36). On the other hand, trustees made enormous mistakes in handling the medical-school proposal. For example, an end-run approach through the legislature was highly unwise. The veto decision by Longley was made less difficult for the Governor because the board and legislators were not willing to compromise by putting the question to referendum, as Longley had requested. In addition, Longley had complained that cost estimates for the project were low, and all indications were that he was correct in drawing that conclusion. A better understanding of the new System could have enhanced the board's credibility during this period, rather than fueling what some Maine citizens perceived as righteous indignation.

Which response level might best diffuse a controversial issue? Which reform proposals might a state legislator choose to support in order to maximize the desired impact? How should a governor evaluate reform options? Strengthening this understanding could enable leaders to achieve greater stability (or, in turn, promote instability) in the environment of higher education governance, both externally and internally. The issue gets to the very heart of the relationship between the state and the public university. In the case of Governor Brennan, a smartly formulated and effective Visiting Committee stemmed a very uneasy time for public higher education in Maine. Despite the roller coaster year of 1986 that included the Jack Freeman resignation, by the end of that year, the higher education community had a solid policy direction and some important new technology funded by a successful bond issue.

Close attention to the results in Part Four allows us to comment on the resiliency of the unified University of Maine System. As can be seen in Table 5.3, the trustees sensed nearly all of the political pressures, and at least some action was taken in every case but one, with the only exception being the Longley request for the board to step down in unison. In some cases, only partial fulfillment of the demands of interveners was authorized, as in the examples of the semi-fulfilled recommendations of the blue-ribbon cost-management study of the 1970s, the supplemental degree-granting nature of the educational network of Maine, and the installation of visiting committees rather than full campus boards. The unified structure's political interfacing mechanisms appeared to greatly soften the blows of controversial issues while requiring action of some sort. In this sense, the structure was flexible enough to prevent possible destruction.

The consistent ability of the unified system to make adjustments for the external environment can be viewed in several ways. Viewed positively, one could first make a case for the unified system as decidedly responsive. It appears plausible that the University of Maine System's ability to adjust preserved its viability as a unified mechanism. In that sense, the System was resilient. This observation is supported by the study for two basic reasons. First, because these major events generated high levels of public controversy, it appeared in several cases that a lack of response by trustees could not have been tolerated politically, and would have led to a dismantling of the System by legislators or the governor, with the full support of the public. The abandonment of the medical-school proposal, the salary and benefits granted to Chancellor Freeman that jumped Maine to the top ten states in administrative compensation, and the attempt to make the educational network a campus of its own were all instances where serious threats to overhaul the System gained likelihood. The evidence from this study demonstrated that action by the Board of Trustees served as a pressure-release valve. At the same time, the ability to make the final decision was not yielded by the Board of Trustees. These events demonstrate a certain balance between the demands of State interests and the desires of public higher education.

Secondly, one might view these interventions negatively, as a sign that a unified system rolls over when pushed by outsiders. In this sense, the University System could be viewed as too pliant. This study concludes, however, that pliancy to political interventions allowed this unified system to remain healthy and intact. In this sense, it passed the test of resiliency. A recent example provides a case in point. Despite an all-out attempt to overhaul the University of Maine System by a private group of citizens led by Owen Wells, Governor Curtis, legislative leaders, and key rank and file legislators, campuses were neither decentralized nor granted full board status. Instead, trustees and the chancellor devised a plan to install visiting boards that would have advisory status, yet improve the ability to assist in fund-raising efforts. This move preserved the control of the trustees and prevented campuses from competing against each other at the executive and legislative branch levels for appropriations. It also sealed the current separation between the agency and State government by not making a more substantive structural change.

A final example underscores a different kind of resiliency. When the ultimate challenge came and Governor Longley asked all trustees to step aside, the System had the legal wherewithal to say no, even to Governor Longley. There was no need to respond to an intervention that did not have state law behind it.

In conclusion, based on all of the observations resulting from the application of this model, the proposition is supported, and the theory that unified governance mechanisms are responsive to political interventions is retained. Using the political intervention model, this paper draws the conclusion that the unified governance system has worked well for Maine in most areas, especially as it relates to the preservation of the System itself. The University of Maine System's unified governance mechanism is effective in adjusting to some of the strongly expressed desires of its citizens. Criticisms have persisted, however, regarding a few programmatic problems. This study concludes that these problems are not beyond the ability of the unified system to respond to them.

Summary of Political Interventions Model

The previous section provided an alternative, factual methodology to identify political interventions using the political interventions model. Individual university decisions were identified from the research and listed in table form. Detailed analysis was provided, specifically addressing the impact of external influencers in order to discover more about whether the state-university relationship in Maine is loosely or tightly coupled. In Maine, it was discovered that there is loose coupling between political interventions and the agency structure. This relationship between the state and the university served as a way for the

System to adjust without the ultimate consequence of suffering unduly or being revamped. In this chapter, the results of the political intervention model are also compared to other findings and analyses; namely, a look back to discern whether the System has achieved what it set out to do.

Responding to the Research Questions
The following four questions were examined during the case-study investigation:
(1) Are government interventions taking place within Maine's unified system of governance?
Not only are interventions taking place in Maine, but they also take place across the nation as well. This question was inserted to initiate the investigation and to clarify the difference between necessary intervention and what some claim is unnecessary intrusion. In Maine, the System has been shown to adjust to political intervention so as to persevere. In other states, the response is different. Study should continue in this area.
(2) If yes, what kind of interventions are taking place? How do they occur?
The major interventions of the past thirty-two years are documented in Table 5.3. Additional intervention attempts are found in other chapters. These interventions appear to occur as a result of statewide public controversies that may get high levels of notoriety and attention in a small state like Maine. In some cases, a governor or the legislature was the intervener, but there were notable exceptions to this circumstance, such as in the case of the University's South African investments.
(3) Does the unified governance system allow for effective interaction between internal university governance and external state involvement?
A major conclusion of this research is that this interaction does exist and is very effective. A unified system (without constitutional provisions) allows for politics to play a role in higher education administration in Maine. For the university administrator, this may look to be unwise. The effectiveness of this System in addressing the needs of Maine citizens may be in

the eye of the beholder. Many in Maine complain about a lack of university accountability, while others are dismayed with the lack of university independence. The research indicates that in terms of the interplay, all is as it should be.
(4) What are some of the resolved and unresolved issues within the University of Maine System that support and/or do not support the unified structure as a model for governance in the age of increasing government interventions?

Resolved issues were detailed in prior chapters. Unresolved programmatic problems were frequently noted in the research and are of future concern to the general stability of this System. It was speculated (but unsubstantiated) that without the tremendous pressure exerted from major attempts at political intervention, some problems that the unified University of Maine System should be dealing with were left open to question. The subject is further complicated by the fact that some of these issues were laid out in the original vision of the founders of the System. Whether these problems are actually caused by a buttress between the wishes of onlookers and the policies of trustees should be the subject of further investigation. This study produced no concrete evidence as to what could be the cause for the shortcoming, but options will be discussed in Chapter 6.

Accountability and Founding Expectations
From the beginning of the effort to create a unified University of Maine System, one of the primary purposes of reorganization was to create an independently managed operation guided by the Chancellor and Board of Trustees. Throughout the 1990s, the value of the independence of the University of Maine System was often questioned.

Has the University of Maine System lived up to the expectation of its founders? You may be surprised by the results of this query. Five key elements were named as advantages of a seamless, coordinated system of higher education, according to the 1966 report entitled "The First Business of Our Times" (State of Maine, 1966).

Advantage #1 was the avoidance of unnecessary duplication of certain education programs. Actual results in this area were mixed, since the goal was to avoid duplicative efforts in higher education, not just within the University of Maine campuses. Campus duplication has been avoided within the System for the most part. However, the Commission on Higher Education Governance did conduct a small survey within its larger study, the results of which were generally unpublished other than within organizational minutes and memoranda. The surveys were forwarded to members of the general public and to university personnel. Frequent responses included "clearer mission statements for the UMS needed" and "Need for a structure to improve coordination between systems," according to a progress report to Commission members (Commission on Higher Education Governance, 1996, February 18). The progress report noted that "Mission statements of the UMS campuses appear to be indistinct and their roles not necessarily reflective of their missions, especially at UMA" (Commission on Higher Education Governance, 1996, February 18). A typical target of critics of the University System over the years was the heavy duplication of courses and programs in teacher education at nearly all campuses. Most studies of the System avoid the issue, however, since the 1986 "Report of the Visiting Committee to the University of Maine" recommended "that the Chancellor and Board of Trustees acknowledge teacher education as one of the most important functions of the University System" (State of Maine, 1986, p. 25). The Commission on Higher Education Governance viewed these problems as more managerial- and mission-related rather than a problem of duplication. Ultimately, the demand appears to justify supply when it comes to replication of programs between university campuses. Unfortunately, duplication between the University of Maine and other public and private institutions has not been avoided.

The Commission strongly recommended better communications between the Maine Technical College System and the University of Maine System to eliminate duplication between the two systems. Part of the rationale for this recommendation appeared to be influenced by other duplication controversies. For example, the University of Maine Board of Trustees' minutes of February 13, 1996, contained the following statement: "There is the potential for duplication of programs, as evidenced by the marine science issue and the community college issue" (Commission on Higher Education Governance, 1996, February 13). Tensions ran high at the Maine Maritime Academy when the University of Maine campus proposed a marine science degree similar to that already offered at Maine Maritime Academy. Unfortunately for Maine

Maritime Academy, the University System undercut an important program without reasonable effort to negotiate an alternative solution. Thus, the overlap between the two public systems was as noticeable as confrontations with the private colleges. It is probable, based on the controversies such as competition with the Husson College nursing program, business administration overlaps, Internet and television outreach, and developments since the medical school veto, that more attention could be focused on the evaluation and necessity of taxpayer-financed programs when private options either exist or could be developed.

Advantage #2 from the 1966 "First Business of Our Times" founding report was the assurance of appropriate duplication of education programs, which appears to be the best reasoning for a plethora of programs in teacher education in Maine, for example. This objective is fully achieved under the unified system. In addition, program outreach into rural Maine counties is rarely questioned.

Advantage #3 from the report was the claim that the broadest variety of educational programs possible would be made available in or close to the centers of population. Two major concerns arise here. First, documentation was available that exposed an under-emphasis on associate-degree offerings. The Commission on Higher Education Governance underscored the problem by posing the question, "Why, if there is plenty of space and ample offerings for AA degrees in the University System, isn't the UMS taking the initiative to work cooperatively with the MTCS?" (State of Maine, 1996, p. ii). Since that statement, the two systems have joined to give associate degree programs another look, but their progress has yet to be scrutinized.

Secondly, the University of Southern Maine (USM), the closest campus to the population centers of greater Portland, lacked a breadth of graduate degree programs and sustained research and development in some important programmatic areas mentioned previously. Doctoral programs were non-existent. This factor alone provides important evidence of systemic shortcomings. The reason behind the slow program growth at USM seems to be shared between two factors. First, the land-grant institution resides in Orono and, as such, it receives the largest share of doctoral and research dollars. Secondly, the 1986 "Report of the Visiting Committee to the University of Maine" recommended that USM be further developed as an "urban comprehensive university" and that

USM "should not embark upon (further) doctoral programs, certainly not at this time" (State of Maine, 1986, p. 21). Although the "Progress Report to the Commission on Higher Education Governance" cited a need for more graduate studies to meet the needs of "place-bound adults desiring career advancement," little has been done (Commission on Higher Education Governance, 1996, February 18, p. 1). Graduate programs are one area where private colleges in Maine see fewer economic benefits in providing opportunities; therefore, it would appear appropriate that the University of Maine System pick up the slack when privates such as the University of New England are unable to meet a need.

Advantage #4 in favor of the unified university system was the avoidance of proliferation of uneconomical, specialized institutions, services, or facilities. Several documented newspaper columns over the years raised the possibility of a merger or elimination of the smallest campus at Fort Kent. A merger of campuses in Fort Kent and Presque Isle was politically difficult to achieve, but one administration for the two campuses under the title "the University of Northern Maine" remained an option. To suggest that this option will cure the woes of the University of Maine System, however, would be a pretense, and a local allegiance to the Fort Kent and Presque Isle programs have made the combination of administrative functions there impossible to achieve.

Although the University of Maine System should be applauded for its proliferation of outreach efforts that include seven campuses, dozens of physical points of contact, and electronic connections, other states have redirected some of these resources into a community college effort. In Maine, the community college offerings are clearly a failure, and in a state with low median family income and a history of comparatively low higher education aspirations, this represents an untenable predicament.

Advantage #5 in favor of establishing the unified system in 1968 was that the transferability of credits would be maximized. This goal has not been completely achieved, but for good reason. Despite the fact that testimony to the Commission on Higher Education Governance lamented that "transferability/applicability of credit continues to be a problem on a statewide basis, and needs to be addressed in some manner by the Commission," evidence emerged that progress on this problem was made in the four years following the Commission's report (State of Maine, 1996, p. 1). Whether it should have taken thirty-two years to make that progress is an altogether different question.

CHAPTER SIX: CONCLUSION

> *The people of Maine are entitled to a master plan that discloses the intentions and purposes of the University of Maine and provides a standard by which progress can be measured.*
>
> Higher Education Planning Commission
>
> in: *Higher Education Planning for Maine*, April 1972, p. 5

Public Accountability and the University of Maine System

It is easy to disagree about the appropriate purpose of various types of university spending. The philosophy behind the spending will always be an easy target. Nevertheless, this research indicated that the Governor and the State Legislature still retain ultimate control over the largest portion of the University of Maine System's budget. At times, large appropriations may have led to poor public accountability for spending, particularly by the end of 1989 when the economy began to turn downward quickly but university spending did not. Complaints to state officials about budget accountability appeared in media outlets both in the early 1980s and early 1990s. Lingering problems such as the transferability of credits issue, over-emphasis on bricks and mortar, the economy, and others aggravated the accountability issue. Regardless of these factors, it is reasonably clear from the wide range of secondary data that the economic downturns that occurred three times (once in each decade) within the research frame virtually guaranteed that public accountability would not be a long-term issue. The rate of spending from State coffers was quickly reduced during hard times by recommendation of each sitting governor and through ratification by the legislature. Some University belt-tightening was apparent following each economic downturn, despite numbers that were characterized by hefty tuition increases. The Maine economy, then, was an external policing mechanism providing public accountability for spending within the University of Maine System, especially since most of the University System's history has seen a heavy reliance on state appropriations, as compared to other sources of revenues. Nevertheless, records regarding the timing of tuition increases indicated that the Board of Trustees might have been among the last people in the state to realize that a recession was underway. The connection between the state's high tuition and the low number of baccalaureate degrees is difficult to refute. In terms of the accountability of the tuition escalations, the System has not performed well.

Although slow to react, the campuses have continued to move forward through the various political climates. Working in conjunction with the authority of the Board of Trustees, campus presidents appeared to be doing an adequate job of preparing students in existing programs to enter the work force. Major program omissions included a low overall level of industry-related research and development, few associate degrees (and even poorer communication of two-year opportunities), the absence of an identity for the community college system, and, in addition, nearly non-existent doctoral offerings near southern population centers. In some specific fields, high-level research was noted. No governor, legislator, or board member played a major leadership role in this arena other than in isolated cases, probably because starting major new programs has high cost barriers. Cost is a major factor inhibiting research and development in this relatively low-income, high-tax-rate, and low-tax-revenue state.

Alumni and fund-raising efforts appeared inadequate in comparison to most other states in the nation. Some recent improvements were noted. The improved level of the endowment is cause for celebration, if not in real terms, at least in an historical context.

Given the current nature of the relationship between the Governor's office and the University of Maine System, it would be possible that a governor of vision could have an impact on private giving. Private citizens of means should not have to confront governors or challenge legislators for more public money, as did happen in Maine when author Stephen King criticized political leaders in the mid-1990s for non-support of the System while pledging one million dollars from his own pocket. Thus far, it appears that Maine's chief executives have failed to harness or cultivate business relationships for higher education's furtherance to any great degree.

In Maine, higher education's heavy reliance on state appropriations means that its future funding will continue to be shaped by the economy, as it has been in the past. The problem exists in other states, but is probably more severe in Maine where a low population supports several campuses and outreach programs. Analysis suggested that until very recently, most states similar in size to Maine had better fund-raising ability and more options for financing to help cushion economic blows.

Governors' Role in Maine Higher Education

Maine Governors since Kenneth Curtis have not dominated the environment for higher education other than the medical-school veto by Governor Longley. In essence, this means that the design is working properly in terms of the provision of decision-making authority to the System's board. Nevertheless, strong Governors have set directions and can make a difference. Governor Curtis proved this by helping to impose radical change through the implementation of the System. Without question, Governor Brennan exerted heavy short-term influence on the University System by way of his depth of involvement with the Visiting Committee and his recommendations for substantive appropriations and a new campus. He may have exerted the most influence on higher education given the statutory constraints that were outlined. Governor McKernan's influence in promoting education to the average and below-average student was revealed as the precursor to today's aspirations initiatives, in that these students were afforded more options for post-secondary opportunity. It also appeared that Governor McKernan's school-to-work approaches broke the old technical college stigma that has been around since "The Yale Report" of 1828, which proclaimed the liberal arts education as all one would need "for any future life" (Whitehead, 1973, p. 126). In fact, linking higher education to economic development continues to be one of today's most powerful movements; apparently in Maine, the perception is that the technical colleges have made the link (better than the University of Maine System, some argue), mostly thanks to Governor McKernan's efforts. Governor King has focused primarily on business and economic needs, but his interest in aspirations gave the higher education community a slight morale boost.

6: Conclusion

Governors of Maine share a bottom-line role in higher education with the legislative branch under current law. They also have the flexibility to set general policy via agency rule-making, although in the case of higher education, almost all major decisions go through the Board of Trustees. The State Board of Education does not play a substantive role in higher education issues. In some cases, governors submit draft legislation, for example, to create study commissions or to perform other functions.

It appears from the historical analysis that future governors may face a functional paralysis in addressing issues of higher education if the trends of higher tuition and low state aid continue to be accompanied by inconsistent fund-raising and haphazard program expansion. In the national literature, the risk of political intrusion is suggested to increase along with these factors; in Maine, the frustration over higher education's dependence on state aid and a natural vulnerability to economic cycles spells difficulty, especially in the likely event of another economic downturn. Other states are experiencing the effects of direct legislative and gubernatorial involvement in areas such as faculty salaries, program offerings, and policy pronouncements. It is very doubtful that University of Maine System's officials, and even Maine people in general, would welcome that brand of involvement, but as we have seen it has occurred in the past.

By far, the most interesting display of gubernatorial power fell within the transition between Governor Longley and Governor Brennan. There is little doubt that Governor Longley was not stymied by the refusal of the trustees to step down. Over time, the governor used his powers to replace board members via the appointment process. One-by-one, new trustees were appointed that shared Longley's philosophy. Many were from southern Maine. Eventually, the shift in the power base was demonstrated by policy changes that favored campuses like the University of Southern Maine over the University of Maine. After Governor Brennan was sworn in, he too appeared to suffer from trustees that were appointed in a previous administration. It is possible that in order to redirect policies back toward the Land Grant institution, the Visiting Committee was hatched. If so, this strategy was both effective and unparalleled.

System Relationship to State Government

Discussion of the adequacy of Maine's governance structure led to changes in the two years leading up to 1999. Although incremental in nature, each change appeared to be designed to deflect existing criticisms and to preserve and protect the advantages of the governance structure as the Board of Trustees and the Chancellor saw it.

The reason most often referred to for establishing the unified approach in 1968 and in preserving the approach today was the fear of what might happen if the campuses had to compete against each other for resources in the legislative arena. In the national literature, this fear appears to be valid in some states and invalid in others. The Michigan approach, for example, thrives in a strongly campus-based format. In Maine, the continued reference to an avoidance of campus competition for funding appeared to be more than simply a scare tactic on the part of the chancellors. Most believed that in a small state like Maine, the resources are too thin to allow government to make allocation decisions beyond the block-grant approach. And with far more legislators hailing from southern Maine, it is interesting to speculate as to the state of university system campuses had there been competition for funding from campus-based boards.

To compensate for the demands for decentralization, complaints about inadequate fund-raising, and other issues, the university system implemented a Board of Visitors at each campus and reintroduced growth in student recruiting after years of down-sizing (documented previously in this report). The new Board of Visitors concept was an obvious effort to get Maine's movers and shakers to become more involved in fund raising without having much influence over programs. Members of Congress, the business community, and others have been appointed to visiting boards at each campus, and results are likely to be positive. However, trustees and the chancellor are surely cognizant that this strategy may lead to the further exclusion of voices; namely, faculty, administrators, students, and parents. If the visiting committees serve to bring more programmatic decisions to the campus and open new lines of communication with faculty and staff, then goals beyond simple funding concerns might be achieved. Unfortunately, more attention paid to each campus through the new involvement of the Visitors may lead to a heightened awareness of campus inadequacies. If, on the other hand, the position is merely ceremonial, the new strategy may not fit within the unified structure's umbrella.

6: *Conclusion*

Implications

Four conclusions were reached in regard to operational tendencies of the current system. First, under the governing-board format used in Maine, it is likely that decision-making power still resides with the Board of Trustees, the Chancellor, and to a lesser extent the campus presidents. Since the arrangement between the Legislature, the Governor, and the University System was formed in 1968, some governors and legislatures have played a role in policy development for the University of Maine System. When political winds blew, results were more expedient. More difficult to assess is the role of the faculty in this power base. While program development has occurred at the University of Maine, other campuses in the System appear to mute the talents of the faculty somewhat, at least in terms of curriculum development. The history of poor labor negotiations is also problematic.

Second, as a result of the centralization of decision-making power, the University of Maine System appears to suffer from an inability to relate to its constituencies. The intensity of this investigation allows us to comment with some surety that the same resiliency that allowed the System to resist the better part of several political intervention attempts over the years also allows it to address university matters whenever trustees see fit. Trustees have the legal wherewithal within the current unified structure to set the agenda for Maine. For example, in effect, the Board has told the people of Maine that the importance of the land-grant and sea-grant status of the University of Maine campus supercedes the founders' system-wide expectation that the broadest variety of educational programs possible would be available nearest the population centers. Alternatively, trustees can argue with credibility that Maine is not big enough to support more than one campus with the vast range of offerings that The University of Maine touts. With the Visiting Committee's report backing their actions, there has been little political impetus for trustees to change their emphasis over the second half of the System's history.

By tracking the board's policy actions and the implications of those actions in this research, it is predictable that the University of Southern Maine will long be the weak stepsister of the University of Maine, until such time as constituents of Southern Maine break down the insulating quality of the unified structure and demand results. Since that has not happened in the first thirty-two years, I do not expect that it will happen

6: Conclusion

over the next thirty-two. Nevertheless, this research proves that political interventions are not only possible, but may be calculated. For the next quarter-century, the University of Southern Maine will continue to hold the potential to be a powerful, full-fledged doctoral-granting university, complete with Division One athletics, performing arts centers, research and development capacity, and the like. While forestry and agriculture expansions may not be in USM's future, the technologies of tomorrow could be.

Third, results to date indicate that while the University System displays a tremendous ability to adjust and persevere, its original goals have not been met after thirty-two years. Despite the high rating in terms of resiliency, the System has not achieved what it set out to do, by virtue of the fact that only three of the original five goals for the System have adequately been met. To reiterate, the University of Maine System has not avoided duplication with the private colleges and Maine Maritime (Advantage #1). It has also failed to offer a broad enough variety of programs at or near its population centers, primarily Southern Maine (Advantage #3). Not only does this region lack proper graduate opportunities in areas such as research and technology, but also library resources are in short supply and the community college option has been in disarray. One might go a step farther and suggest that at the very least, the University of Southern Maine should maintain its own board of trustees. In another state, such an institution would be a state university or state college, and it would come complete with top-rated scholarship, facilities, and Division-One athletics. The City of Portland's future and the region itself may suffer unknowingly as a result of this consequence.

A second logical direction for the state would be to separate the community college component from the System Board of Trustees. This failed experiment now enters its third decade, and with no organized group support, political intervention is extremely unlikely. Will a new shared arrangement with the technical colleges encounter success?

Governor Ken Curtis, the System's founding governor, understands that these key expectations have not been met. Now in his 70s, Governor Curtis maintains the youthful enthusiasm for higher education that he had when he served Maine during the System's formation in the 1960s. He believes that the time has come to decentralize the unified system, not because the system responds to political intervention, but because in spite of this, he believes that the key expectations of the founders are still

6: Conclusion

relevant today. But a relevant response to this topic has been, so what? The University of Maine System continues to be a tremendous asset for the State of Maine. Acknowledging the bumps in the road, the literature reflects a system that Maine citizens can be proud of, in spite of its limited resources.

The fourth and final conclusion is that the University of Maine System's structure is resilient. Each political intervention of consequence was dealt with, regardless of opinion about the sluggish nature of trustee decision-making. This finding leads to a recommendation that other states carefully examine Maine as a system of higher education that affords a balance between government intervention and institutional autonomy.

Some weaknesses are apparent. Questions left at the foot of this research might leave some Maine people surprised. For example, how can a well-designed structure that can withstand serious political interventions not be living up to the goals and expectations of its founders? While goals can and should change, are the original goals obsolete, or just ignored? Does the voluntary nature and infrequent meetings of the Board of Trustees allow them to fully exercise their leadership role? Could another structural format (or an adjustment in the current mechanism) have adapted to political interventions while also achieving the founder's goals? More importantly, armed with a better knowledge about what works and what doesn't in Maine's unified system, what will the disposition of the next Maine government be to the educational needs of Maine citizens?

REFERENCES

Allen, T. (1990, December 16). Chancellor says cuts will hit university hard. *Sunday Sun Journal,* p. 1D.

Associated Press. (1975, October 1). Longley wants schools to compete for funds. *Portland Press Herald,* p. 1.

Associated Press. (1995, December 16). MacTaggart emerges as top choice. *Portland Press Herald,* p. 5B.

Bailey, D. (1983, November 6). McCarthy resignation fallout. *Maine Sunday Telegram,* p. 15A.

Balogh, C.P. (1993). *Higher education, autonomy, and corporate academic freedom in Florida: A legislative analysis.* Unpublished doctoral dissertation, The Florida State University.

Balancing the trustees. (1984, June 13). *Bangor Daily News,* p. 14.

Ballard, S. (1997, May). *The social responsibility of the public university: building partnerships with state government.* Paper presented at LINKS 97 Conference, Springfield, IL.

Beeny, S. (1974, December 10). Freeman, McNeil deputy, acting chancellor of UM. *Portland Press Herald,* p. 1.

Big plans. (1985, November 23). *Bangor Daily News,* p. 22.

Board of Trustees of the University of Maine System. (1969, December 18). *Minutes.* Bangor, ME: Author.

Board of Trustees of the University of Maine System. (1970, April 10). *Minutes.* Bangor, ME: Author.

Board of Trustees of the University of Maine System. (1970, September 28). *Minutes.* Bangor, ME: Author.

Board of Trustees of the University of Maine System. (1972, November 9). *Minutes.* Bangor, ME: Author.

Board of Trustees of the University of Maine System. (1986, August 25). *Minutes.* Bangor, ME: Author.

Board of Trustees of the University of Maine System. (1986, November 24). *Minutes.* Bangor, ME: Author.

Board of Trustees of the University of Maine System. (1987, March 26). *Minutes.* Bangor, ME: Author.

Board of Trustees of the University of Maine System. (1987, July 20). *Minutes*. Bangor, ME: Author.
Board of Trustees of the University of Maine System. (1987, November 16). *Minutes*. Bangor, ME: Author.
Board of Trustees of the University of Maine System. (1988, January 25). *Minutes*. Bangor, ME: Author.
Board of Trustees of the University of Maine System. (1990, November 12). *Minutes*. Bangor, ME: Author.
Board of Trustees of the University of Maine System. (1990, December 17). *Minutes*. Bangor, ME: Author.
Board of Trustees of the University of Maine System. (1992). *Positioning the University of Maine System for the 21st Century: Project 2002*. Bangor, ME: Patricia Collins, ad Hoc Committee Chair.
Board of Trustees of the University of Maine System. (1996, September 30). *Minutes*. Bangor, ME: Author.
Board of Trustees of the University of Maine System. (1996, November 18). *Minutes*. Bangor, ME: Author.
Board of Trustees of the University of Maine System. (1997, January 27). *Minutes*. Bangor, ME: Author.
Board of Trustees of the University of Maine System. (1997, September 22). *Minutes*. Bangor, ME: Author.
Board of Trustees of the University of Maine System. (1997, November 10). *Minutes*. Bangor, ME: Author.
Bowen, F. M., Bracco, K. R., Callan, P. M., Finney, J. E., Richarson, R. C. Jr., & Trombley, W. (1997). *State structures for the governance of higher education: A comparative study* (Report No. 9-11). San Jose, CA: California Higher Education Policy Center.
Brennan, J. E. (1983, February 22). *State of the State Address by Governor Joseph E. Brennan,* Presented at the Joint Convention of the 111th Maine State Legislature, Augusta, ME.
Brennan, J. E. (1984, January 31). *State of the State Address by Governor Joseph E. Brennan,* Presented at the Joint Convention of the 111th Maine State Legislature, Augusta, ME.
Brennan, J. E. (1985, January 31). *State of the State Message of Joseph E. Brennan, Governor of Maine,* Presented at the Joint Convention of the 112th Maine State Legislature, Augusta, ME.

References

Brennan, J. E. (1986, January 21). *State of the State Message of Joseph E. Brennan, Governor of Maine,* Presented at the Joint Convention of the 112th Maine State Legislature, Augusta, ME.

Brennan, J. E. (1986, March 20). *Address on Higher Education of Joseph E. Brennan, Governor of Maine,* Presented at the Joint Convention of the 112th Maine State Legislature, Augusta, ME.

Brewer, P. (1992, August 5). UM system 10-year plan stresses quality for less. *Aroostook Republican and News,* p. 7A.

Brown, C. M. (1993). *Governance of higher education in Louisiana: The process and impact of politics.* Unpublished doctoral dissertation, The Florida State University.

Carlisle, P. S., Wells, O. W., & Fitzgerald, D. D. (1996). *The University of Maine System: A time of a change.* Unpublished Manuscript.

Carnegie Commission on Higher Education. (1973). *Governance of higher education.* New York: McGraw-Hill.

Carrier, P. (1996, November 17). Curtis joins critics of university system. *Maine Sunday Telegram,* pp. 1B, 12B.

Chancellor McCarthy to quit UMaine in '86. (1985, July 23). *Morning Sentinel,* p. 5.

Cheever, D. (1997, January 1). UM system to shed 120 tenured profs. *Kennebec Journal,* p. 1.

Cohen, T. (1995, December 26). New Chancellor adept at handling tough issues. *Portland Press Herald,* pp. 1A, 14A.

Commission on Higher Education Governance. (1996, February 13). *Minutes.* Augusta, ME: Author.

Commission on Higher Education Governance. (1996, February 18). *Progress report and interview responses.* Augusta, ME: Otteson.

Cowley, W. H. (1980). *Presidents, professors, and trustees.* San Francisco: Jossey Bass.

Curran, J. (1990, June 27). More layoffs planned at UMaine. *Bangor Daily News,* p. 7.

Curtis, K. M. (1967, January 26). *Special message on human and cultural resources,* Presented to the One Hundred and Third Legislature, Augusta, ME.

Curtis, K. M. (1969, January 9). *Budget message address,* Presented to the One Hundred and Fourth Legislature, Augusta, ME.

Curtis, K. M. (1969, February 11). *Special message on education*, Presented to the One Hundred and Fourth Legislature, Augusta, ME.
Curtis, K. M. (1971, January 13). *Budget message address*, Presented to the One Hundred and Fifth Legislature, Augusta, ME.
Day, J. S. (1975, February 15). UM trustees asked again to step down. *Bangor Daily News*, p. 1.
Day, J. S. (1975, March 8). Longley scores UM official for 'scare tactics.' *Bangor Daily News*, p. 13.
Don't splinter the system. (1974, December 20). *Portland Press Herald*, p. 10.
Dowd, M. (1990, May 22). Trustees' policy supports UMS athletics. *Bangor Daily News*, p. 17.
Dr. Oliver Cope named to aid McNeil in planning for UM medical school. (1972, March 16). *Portland Press Herald*, p. 14.
Dugas, S. B. (1994). *Support for higher education in the 1992-1993 Louisiana Legislature.* Unpublished doctoral dissertation, The Louisiana State University and Agricultural and Mechanical College.
Easton, D. (1965). *A framework for political analysis.* Englewood Cliffs, NJ: Prentice-Hall.
End of search. (1975, June 28). *Portland Press Herald*, p. 24.
Forkey, B. (1985, August 25). Taking a hard look at the University of Maine. *Maine Sunday Telegram*, p. 19A.
Forkey, B. (1986, June 9). Freeman pay ranks him ninth in nation. *Portland Press Herald*, p. 1.
Forkey, B. (1986, July 17). Disillusioned chancellor quits. *Portland Press Herald*, p. 1
Freeman resignation. (1986, July 18). *Lewiston Sun Journal*, p. 6A.
Garber, A. (1997, October 26). UMaine loses students as USM swells. *Maine Sunday Telegram*, pp. B1, B16.
Garber, A. (1999, June 17). Growth puzzles UMaine system. *Portland Press Herald*, p. 1A.
Garber, A. (1999, July 11). Chancellor quietly works out the kinks. *Portland Press Herald*, p. 1A.
Garland, N. (1986, May 20). Trustees OK $114,000 salary for Freeman. *Bangor Daily News*, pp. 1-2.
Garland, N. (1986, May 21). New chancellor state's highest paid public official. *Bangor Daily News*, p. 7.

Garland, N. (1986, July 24). Curtis proposed for top UMS job. *Bangor Daily News*, pp. 1-2.

Garland, N. (1986, August 6). Fast-paced chancellor's search a concern to some lawmakers. *Bangor Daily News*, p. 1.

Garland, N. (1986, October 23). Chancellor, UM president explain $7.7 million bond issue. *Bangor Daily News*, p. 20.

Goodman, D. (1995, March 26). University chancellor barraged by faculty. *Boston Globe*, p. 41.

Haimila, S. (1977, December 16). Chancellor hit at UMA meeting. *Kennebec Journal*, p. 17.

Hale, J. (1995, March 3). UMS chancellor makes call for restructuring. *Bangor Daily News*, p. A1.

Hale, K. K. (1991, April 26). Chancellor prods legislature to OK tax increase. *Kennebec Journal*, p. 5.

Hale, K. K. (1995, March 14). Petition calls for no-confidence vote on UMaine's chancellor. *Kennebec Journal*, p. 1.

Hansen, D. (1972, January 21). UM official defends cost of McNeil's Office. *The Portland Press Herald*, p. 30.

Harkavy, J. (1974, February 9). UM's McNeil dreams of minimal tuition by 1980. *The Portland Press Herald*, p. 22.

Heindle, E. K. B. (1993). *An overview of the Mississippi Legislature and Mississippi public senior institutions of higher learning.* Unpublished doctoral dissertation, The University of Mississippi.

Hertz, B. (1972, January 31). University gets taxpayer heel. *The Bangor Daily News*, pp. 1, 2.

Hertz, B. (1972, February 1). UMO's chancellor: What's his job? *The Bangor Daily News*, pp. 1, 3.

Hertz, B. (1972, February 2). Some questions, some answers. *The Bangor Daily News*, pp. 1, 3.

Hertz, B. (1972, February 4). Super university resistance still a factor on campuses, *The Bangor Daily News*, p. 1.

Higher Education Planning Commission. (1972, April). *Higher education planning for Maine.* Portland, ME: Coffin, F. M., Chairman.

High stakes poker. (1975, March 8). *Kennebec Journal*, p. 4.

Himmelstein, D. (1983, December 4). UMaine reform bill meets opposition. *Portland Press Herald*, p. 25.

Hines, E. R. (1988). *Higher education and state governments: Renewed partnership, cooperation, or competition?* ASHE-ERIC Higher Education Report No. 5. Washington, DC: Association for the Study of Higher Education.

Hoff, P. S. (1997). *Back to the future: The University of Maine and its land grant/sea grant tradition.* Orono, ME: University of Maine, Office of the President.

Hoff, P. S. (1998, February 23). *BearWorks.* Orono, ME: University of Maine, Office of President.

Hook, S., Kurtz, P., & Todorovich, M. (Eds.). (1978). *The university and the state: What role for government in higher education?* Buffalo, New York: Prometheus Books.

Hot seat. (1980, April 7). *Bangor Daily News,* p. 10.

Hutchinson, F. E. (1993). *University of Maine preliminary downsizing proposal.* Orono, ME: University of Maine, Office of the President.

Irwin, C. T. (1977, January 2). UM study examines future direction. *Maine Sunday Telegram,* p. 3.

Jacobson, G., Norton, N., Markowsky, G., Hunter, M., & Smith, D. (1997). *Higher education in Maine.* Orono, ME: University of Maine.

Katz, B. (1995, November 15). University loses race of priorities [Viewpoint]. *Kennebec Journal,* p. 6.

Kesseli, D. (1993, November 16). UMS chancellor Orenduff relishes the job ahead. *Bangor Daily News,* p. 1. Ketchum (1987). *Internal review and assessment of development capabilities and external planning study for $25,000,000 capital campaign.* Boston, MA: Author.

King, Jr., A. S. (1995, February 1). *Budget in brief: summary of the program and budget proposals for fiscal years 1996-1997.* Augusta, ME.

King, Jr., A. S. (1997). *Budget in brief: summary of the program and budget proposals for fiscal years 1998-1999.* Augusta, ME.

Krause, D. S., Sloan, J., Jagermann, R. W., Bernier, R. E., Katz, J. A., Kuratko, D. F., & Engeleiter, S. A. (1990, Fall). Can academia truly help small business owners? *Small Business Forum,* 1-8.

Larrabee, D. (1976, March 13). Tax boost injurious, claims Longley. *Bangor Daily News,* P. 25.

Lawrence, M. W., & Jacobson, G. L. (1997). Jumpstart 2000--The Maine economic improvement strategy: A targeted investment in research and development. *Maine Policy Review, 6* (1), pp. 35-43.
Lee, L. C., & Bowen, F. M. (1971). *The multicampus university.* New York: McGraw-Hill.
Libby, W. (1973, October 3). Super-U's future: time for leadership. *The Bangor Daily News.* p. 18.
Lindzey, G. & Aronson, E. (Eds.) (1968). *The handbook of social psychology.* Reading, MA: Addison Wesley.
Longley again defends budget, suggests UM trustees unfair. (1975, March 29). *Portland Press Herald,* p. 26.
Longley, J. B. (1977). *Budget message address,* Presented to the One Hundred and Eighth Legislature, Augusta, ME.
MacTaggart, T. (1997, February). *Report to the Maine State Legislature.* Presented at the Joint Convention of the 118th Maine State Legislature, Augusta, ME.
MacTaggart, T. J. & Associates. (1998). *Seeking excellence through independence.* San Francisco: Jossey-Bass.
Maine Senate. (1975, June 17). *Legislative record* (B2037). Augusta, ME.
Maraghy, G. (1975, July 6). UM chancellor is tough, jovial planner, educator. *Maine Sunday Telegram,* p. 1.
Maraghy, G. (1975, December, 4). Times tough, UM board puts hold on enrollment. *Portland Press Herald,* p. 1.
Margaret Chase Smith Center for Public Policy. (1997). *Strategic environmental assessment of the University of Maine System.* Orono, ME: University of Maine.
Mavrinac/Marsh Consultants with Mallar Development Services, Inc., (1982). *Planning for the 80's: Post secondary education and the Maine economy.* Augusta, ME.
McCall, S. (1995, April 3). Orenduff resigns as UMaine chancellor. *Portland Press Herald,* p. 1A.
McCarthy insists UM well-managed school. (1977, February 8). *Portland Press Herald,* p. 1.
McGuinness, A. C. Jr. (1994). *The changing structure of higher education leadership.* Manuscript submitted for publication. National Center for Higher Education Management Systems, Boulder, CO.

McKernan, Jr., J. R. (1987, February 5). *Budget Address of John R. McKernan, Jr., Seventieth Governor of Maine.* Presented at the Joint Convention of the 113th Maine State Legislature, Augusta, ME.

McKernan, Jr., J. R. (1989, January). *Continuing the Commitment: Summary of Program and Budget Proposals for the Fiscal Years 1990-1991.* Augusta, ME.

McKernan, Jr., J. R. (1989, January 26). *State of the State Address of John R. McKernan, Jr.,* Presented at the Joint Convention of the 114th Maine State Legislature, Augusta, ME.

McKernan, Jr., J. R. (1990, January 25). *State of the State Address of John R. McKernan, Jr.,* Presented at the Joint Convention of the 114th Maine State Legislature, Augusta, ME.

McKernan, Jr., J. R. (1992, January 15). *State of the State Address of John R. McKernan, Jr.,* Presented at the Joint Convention of the 115th Maine State Legislature, Augusta, ME.

McKernan, Jr., J. R. (1994). *Making the Grade.* Boston, MA: Little, Brown & Co.

National Center for Higher Education Management Systems. (1995). *The changing structure of state higher education leadership.* Boulder, CO: McGuinness.

National Commission on Excellence in Education. (1983). *A nation at risk.*

Washington, D.C.

Neavoll, G. (1996, November 24). UMaine system needs a Curtis Commission. *Maine Sunday Telegram,* p. 4C.

Newman, F. (1987). *Choosing quality.* Denver, CO: Education Commission of the States.

Newman, F. (1987 A). *Higher education and the American resurgence.* Carnegie Foundation Special Report, Lawrenceville, NJ: Princeton University Press.

Norton, M. (1990, December 11). UM says it can't meet budget target. *Portland Press Herald,* p. 10A.

Norton, M. (1991, July 21). UMaine system displays few scars. *Maine Sunday Telegram,* p. 1B.

Novak, C. (1995). Interview with John R. McKernan, Jr. *Technos Quarterly, 4* (1).

Orenduff, M. J. (1993). *The chancellor's report*. (Price, K. A., Ed.). Bangor, ME: University of Maine System.

Palm, K. (1975, February 14). UM trustees turn down Longley'e resignation plea. *Portland Press Herald*, p. 36.

Perry, N. (1990, February 11). UMaine chief 'a lightning rod.' *Maine Sunday Telegram*, p. 1.

Perry, N. (1990, August 1). State forced to delay payment to UMaine. *Morning Sentinal*, p. 3.

Perry, N. (1996, September 29). King balks as university system aggressively seeks more state aid. *Maine Sunday Telegram*, pp. 1A, 8A.

Perry, N. (1996, December 8). State's top scholars pass up Umaine. *Maine Sunday Telegram*, P. 1B.

Peterson, M. W. (1985). Emerging developments in postsecondary organization theory and research: Fragmentation and integration. *Educational Researcher, 14* (3) pp. 5-12.

P. L. 1995, Chapter 395, Part Q, M.R.S.A.

Rawson, D. (1986, January 15). Legislators say recommendations better than trustee's plan. *Bangor Daily News*, p. 16.

Reilly, W. (1975, September 4). UM chancellor urges more services for public. *Bangor Daily News*, p. 17.

Reilly, W. (1976, February 4). UM chancellor launches campaign for $6.4 million. *Bangor Daily News*, p. 15.

Reilly, W. (1976, August 26). Super U under fire. *Bangor Daily News*, pp. 1, 2.

Rcilly, W. (1978, April 13). Longley's effect on Super-U to outlive term. *Bangor Daily News*, p. 1

Reilly, W. (1978, May 12). Union representation chosen by UM faculty. *Bangor Daily News*, p. 1.

Reilly, W. (1978, November 18). UM faculty demands focus on money, decision making. *Bangor Daily News*, p. 31.

Reilly, W. (1981, March 17). UM student cite transfer problem. *Bangor Daily News*, p. 1.

Reilly, W. (1981, September 30). McCarthy cites rise in UM faculty pay. *Bangor Daily News*, p. 11.

Reilly, W. (1982, July 27). University votes divestiture of investments in S. Africa. *Bangor Daily News*, p. 1.

Reilly, W. (1990, November 29). UM faculty criticism targets president Dale Lick. *Bangor Daily News,* p. 5.

Rooks, D. (1999, March 18). A partnership, not a system. *Maine Times,* pp. 3-7.

Rosenfeld, S. (1976, April 1). Longley relaxes stance on aid for university. *Portland Press Herald,* p. 1.

Schick, E. B., Novak, R. J., Norton, J. A., & Elam, H. G. (1992). *Shared visions of public higher education governance: Structures and leadership styles that work.* Washington, DC: American Association of State Colleges and Universities.

Shugar, S. R. (1994). *The relationship between public higher education governance systems and the perceptions of high-echelon administrators.* Unpublished doctoral dissertation, Northern Illinois University.

Silvernail, D. L. (1997). Increasing postsecondary enrollments in Maine. *Maine Policy Review, 6,* p. 27.

Skelton, K. (1998, August 20). Is bigger better? *Maine Times,* p. 4.

State of Maine. (1966). *The first business of our times.* Augusta, ME: McCain, J. A., Chairman.

State of Maine. (1986). *Report of the Visiting Committee to the University of Maine.* Augusta, ME: Strider, R.E.L.

State of Maine. (1988, July 1). *The Governor's human resource development plan.* Augusta, ME: Office of the Governor.

State of Maine. (1990). *Report of the commission to assess the impact of increased state spending on the University of Maine System.* Augusta, ME: Office of Fiscal and Program Review.

State of Maine. (1996). *Report of the commission on higher education governance.* Augusta, ME: Office of Policy and Legal Analysis.

State of Maine. (1999). *Compendium of state fiscal information.* Augusta, ME: Office of Fiscal and Program Review.

Steele, J. (1974, November 7). No intention of resigning, *The Bangor Daily News.* p. 21.

Steel, J. (1975, May 21). University's med-school lobbying fraud on taxpayers, Longley says. *Bangor Daily News,* p. 31.

Steel, J. (1975, June 5). UM candidate: stretch dollars. *Bangor Daily News,* p. 17.

References

Troyer, K. (1993, April 27). Woodbury to quit after seven years as UMaine chancellor. *Portland Press Herald*, p. 1A.

20-A Maine Revised Statutes Annotated, Chapter 409, s 10701-10714.

20-A Maine Revised Statutes Annotated, Chapter 411, s 10901-10907.

20-A Maine Revised Statues Annotated, Cumulative Pocket Supplement, Chapter 431-A, s 12705-12714 (1994).

UMaine growth: loose controls, planning. (1986, March 2). *Maine Sunday Telegram*, p. 17A.

UMO newspaper cites austerity budget's effects. (1976, October 14). *Portland Press Herald*, p. 1.

University of Maine. (1995, November 1-2). *Assessing the environment for public higher education in Maine*. Unpublished Manuscript, University of Maine.

University of Maine System. (1985). *The University and the future: The reports of a series of task forces addressing the major issues facing the University of Maine*. Bangor, ME: Office of Finance and Treasurer.

University of Maine System. (1995). *Financial overview of the University of Maine System: chart package*. Bangor, ME: Office of Finance and Treasurer.

U. of M. takes steps toward saving money. (1975, February 14). *Portland Press Herald*, p. 36.

Vamvakias, S. G. (1997, December 11). Making college accessible. *The Portland Press Herald*, p. A17.

Vanderweide, H. (1975, March 20). UM independence called vital in fulfilling needs. *Portland Press Herald*, p. 33.

Warner, p. (1994, April 1). Report generates only mild reaction. *Bangor Daily News*, p. 9.

Whitehead, J. S. (1973). *The separation of college and state*. New Haven, CT: Yale University Press.

Wilson, E., & Call, M. (1985). *The laws of the State of Maine affecting the University of Maine*. Augusta, ME: State Law Library.

Wilson, R. (1990, February 23). Squandering the down payment. *Maine Times*, pp. 14-16.

Woodbury, R. L. (1986, February 9). Report didn't capture USM's reality and dreams. *Sunday Sun-Journal*, p. 3D.

Woodbury, R. L. (1992). *The chancellor's report*. (Price, K. A., Ed.). Bangor, ME: University of Maine System.

Woodbury, R. L. (1993, February). *State of the University of Maine System*. Presented at the Joint Convention of the 118th Maine State Legislature, Augusta, ME.

Yin, R. K. (1994). *Case study research*. Thousand Oaks, CA: SAGE.

Young, C. (1995, January 22). ITV plan gets static from faculty. *Sunday Sun-Journal*, p. A3.

Young, S. (1995, April 6). Ex-UMS chief returns. *Bangor Daily News*, p. A3.

Young, S. (1997, February 1). Plethora of bills set to overhaul UMaine system. *Bangor Daily News*, pp. A1, A8.

Young, S. (1997, July 12). UMS revamping comes up short. *Bangor Daily News*, pp. B1, B8.

APPENDIX A

Transcript of Governor Longley Veto Statement for University Medical School

June 16, 1975

To the Honorable Members of the House of Representatives and the Senate of the 107th Maine Legislature:

A great American, whom I admire, kept a saying on his desk: "The buck stops here." Since this Legislature, after a back-and-forth debate, has seen fit to place the key decision regarding the future of a medical school for Maine in my hands, I accept the consequences of an extremely difficult choice. I am vetoing L. D. 773, An Act to Authorize the University of Maine to Proceed with the Development of a School of Medicine as Part of the Teaching Program of the University System.

I therefore request in the interests of fiscal responsibility and to avoid a recurrence of an L. D. 1994 type situation, as well as to help restore our favorable bond rating, that you sustain this veto.

While I had previously indicated my opposition to a medical school, my respect of the Legislature and my desire to be fair to proponents and the University caused me to step back and spend countless hours of my own time plus that of my staff and volunteer citizens in reevaluating the total situation. As a result of this time and research, I am electing to veto this bill because of the following specific reasons:

1. The Legislature had passed and sent to the Governor a bill that calls for a substantial present and future commitment of the state's resources to the establishment of a medical school, while failing to appropriate the funds necessary to accomplish this purpose. In other words, the Legislature has not appropriated any money in the current services budget to pay for the school. Approval of this bill could mean a further erosion of already tight operating funds or a future tax increase. Furthermore, this Governor can ill afford the luxury of approving bills that have been submitted to him without an allocation of cost or appropriation by the Legislature. Furthermore, as a result of my

experience as Governor, I do not want to be unfair to future Governors or Legislatures and approve bills without appropriate costs or price tags. This Legislature and this Governor have paid the price of this approach.

2. The cost estimates presented by proponents of the school are not realistic, and fail to project costs to the State of Maine for adequate faculty, future building, and/or capital equipment needs, as well as costs to the state in the event that federal funds are eliminated or cut back. I have a strong feeling that Maine cannot afford in the future another cost estimate mistake such as occurred with L. D. 1994. This could also happen here.

3. There was no conclusive evidence presented that shows that a medical school will solve Maine's doctor shortage in rural areas. It is my understanding that many of the more expert in the medical and health care fields believe that the solution to the doctor shortage in Maine lives in the development of residency programs, and not a medical school. Further, we should in this regard improve our efforts to aid new doctors in overcoming the many difficulties associated with the establishment of practices in rural areas.

4. As Governor, I want to help the University. However, to add an additional burden involving program and finances could severely hinder the University at this time. There is some evidence already that time and dollars spent promoting and lobbying for a medical school have hurt the present University program and budget.

In addition, I have strong reservations about the form of this legislation in that the medical school would come under the jurisdiction of the present Board of Trustees of the University of Maine, which I feel has its hands full getting its own financial house in order.

5. I am also advised that additional spaces are available for our medical students at out-of-state institutions and much lower costs would be possible utilizing these programs. Statistics also show that 54.2 percent of Maine residents who graduated from the University of Vermont School of Medicine under the Regional Medical Student Program, administered by the New England Board of Higher Education, returned to Maine to practice medicine during the years from 1958 to 1973. Our research also indicates that proponents either did not understand or failed to recognize and report this fact, plus evidence that the University of Vermont and other medical schools will now be able to accept more Maine students. Ironically, and unfortunately, Maine's

Appendix A: Governor Longley Veto Statement 175

gain in this regard is Massachusetts' loss, as these additional openings reportedly are primarily attributable to that state's financial problems, which were caused in part when costs associated with the University of Massachusetts medical school mushroomed beyond cost projections promulgated by those who promoted the School. This is because Massachusetts has indicated that due to its financial crisis and cost overruns on its medical school, it is going to have to use funds to support its medical school, as contrasted with supporting students in other medical schools.

Even though I am vetoing this measure, I pledge:

A. To conduct an intensive campaign to attract and retain doctors in Maine.

B. To attempt to locate resources to subsidize doctors and other health care professionals in our rural areas.

C. To proceed immediately with New Hampshire and Vermont to explore the possibility of developing a regional medical school facility and program.

D. To continue efforts already started to get doctors to move to Maine's rural areas from other states. I have already made initial contact with medical schools and the Maine Medical Association in this regard.

E. We should also explore the possibility of asking one of our fine private institutions to develop a medical education program. This would protect the University from further erosion of its undergraduate efforts and also give the taxpayers the advantage of the greater budgetary scrutiny that occurs in the private-college sector, which contrasts with the tendency of a state university to go to the taxpayers whenever it makes a mistake or needs money.

While realizing that many members supported the medical school legislation in good faith, for the above reasons, I respectfully ask that my veto be sustained.

Very truly yours,

James B. Longley, Governor

APPENDIX B

Transcript of Chancellor Freeman's Letter to Governor Brennan, July 1986

Dear Joe:

It is with sincere regret that I hereby tender my resignation as Chancellor of the University of Maine System, effective immediately.

The reasons for my decision are complex. After two weeks of intensive review of the financial and academic condition of the system, and the political and economic climate in Maine, I have reluctantly concluded that the high goals enunciated by the Visiting Committee and endorsed by the Board are probably not attainable within the resources likely to be available now and in the future. I, frankly, am disillusioned by the general climate of public opinion in Maine in respect to the University System as manifested in the public outcry over my salary, and that of Dr. Lick; and the threats from some quarters to 'punish' the Board and the University by denying approval of a badly needed, quite modest, and fully justifiable bond issue; and the intense politicization of even minor issues at the University. I also am concerned about the obvious reluctance of some members of the board, the legislature, and the general public to provide minimally competitive salaries to dedicated faculty and administrators. I am simply not comfortable with the way that business is done in Maine, and I fear that I will become increasingly disenchanted with the situation were I to remain.

Inasmuch as I have not yet moved my family from Pittsburgh and my former position at Pitt is still available to me, I have decided, after much deliberation, to reverse my decision to come to Maine while I still can. While I probably should have made this decision before accepting the position in May, since I have had some of these concerns for some time, I rationalized that things would turn out well. Unfortunately, my concerns have only deepened with time. It seems best for all concerned, therefore, that I withdraw, before becoming even more committed to a situation that is unlikely to work out well for me or the University.

Joe, I most sincerely regret the difficulties that my decision may create for you and the Board, who have been creative, candid, courageous, and generous in support of my candidacy. In all candor, however, I believe that a decision on my part to remain, feeling as I do, would only generate more problems for everyone in the long run.

I thank you and the Board for your confidence and consideration. You have my most sincere best wishes in your valiant efforts to improve the system of higher education in Maine.

APPENDIX C

PORTRAITS OF GOVERNORS AND CHANCELLORS

PRESIDING OVER THE

UNIVERSITY OF MAINE SYSTEM

Appendix C: Portraits of Governors and Chancellors   181

(Source: Maine Archives)
Governor Kenneth M. Curtis

Appendix C: Portraits of Governors and Chancellors

(Source: Maine Archives)

Governor James B. Longley

Appendix C: Portraits of Governors and Chancellors 183

(Source: Maine Archives)
Governor Joseph E. Brennan

184   *Appendix C: Portraits of Governors and Chancellors*

(Source: Maine Archives)

Governor John R. McKernan, Jr.

Appendix C: Portraits of Governors and Chancellors   185

(Source: Maine Archives)

Governor Angus S. King, Jr.

186   *Appendix C: Portraits of Governors and Chancellors*

(Source: University of Maine System)

Chancellor Donald R. McNeil

Appendix C: Portraits of Governors and Chancellors 187

(Source: University of Maine System)
Chancellor Patrick E. McCarthy

188   *Appendix C: Portraits of Governors and Chancellors*

(Source: Portland Press Herald [Author's Note: The University of Maine System does not keep a photograph of Chancellor Freeman on file.])

Chancellor Jack E. Freeman

Appendix C: Portraits of Governors and Chancellors   189

(Source: University of Maine System)
Chancellor Robert L. Woodbury

190   *Appendix C: Portraits of Governors and Chancellors*

(Source: Portland Press Herald [Author's Note: The University of Maine System does not keep a photograph of Chancellor Orenduff on file.])

Chancellor J. Michael Orenduff

Appendix C: Portraits of Governors and Chancellors

(Source: University of Maine System)
Chancellor Terrence MacTaggart

Biography of the Author

The Honorable James D. Libby was born in Saco, Maine on November 14, 1960. He was raised in Buxton, Maine and graduated from Bonny Eagle High School in 1979. He attended Nasson College and graduated with a Bachelor of Science degree in Business Administration in 1983. He received a Master of Business Administration degree from Saint Bonaventure University in 1985, and a Certificate of Advanced Study degree in educational administration from The University of Maine in 1996. In 2000 he earned a Doctor of Philosophy degree in Public Policy from the University of Maine.

Jim is a second-term State Senator. He has served in the past as an Assistant Professor of Business Administration and a Department Chair at Saint Joseph's College in Maine, where he also participated as an assistant coach in two NAIA men's national basketball championship tournaments. He has also served on several boards and commissions in Maine, including the Maine Labor Relations Board and the Maine Committee on Global Education. He was a panel member at Maine's Higher Education Summit. Senator Libby has also served two terms in Maine's House of Representatives, and is a former member of the Legislature's Joint Standing Committee on Education and Cultural Affairs. He holds a State of Maine Certification as a Superintendent of Schools.

His hobbies are basketball, golf, canoeing, and cribbage. He resides in Buxton with his wife Jenny.

EVERY NAME INDEX

The following Every Name Index contains a total of 227 entries. Names found in reference citations have not been indexed.

Albanese
 J Duke, 114
Alfond
 Harold, 91
Baldacci
 John, 83-84, 86, 88, 143
Ballard
 Steve, 96
Barringer
 Richard, 88
Brennan
 Joseph E, 46, 56, 69, 72, 76, 78, 80, 82, 84, 93, 144, 156, 183
Brown
 Ada, 83
 Francis, 87
 Prof David, xiii
Bustin
 David, 144
Butland
 Jeffrey, 129-130
Cameron
 James, 108
Carlisle
 Peter, 111, 119
Childs

Jean, 76
Cobb
 Dean Robert, xiii
Collins
 Patricia, 108
Connick
 George, 109
Cope
 Oliver, 59
Curtis
 Kenneth M, 46-51, 86, 88, 111, 128, 141-142, 155, 159, 181
Diamond
 John, 87
Dionne
 Paul, 80
Dodge
 Clayton, 83
Fitzgerald
 Duane, 119
Flanagan
 David, 83
Fournier
 Norman, 119
Freeman

Jack E, 46, 56-60, 82-83, 86, 140-145, 177, 188
 Stanley L, 46, 56, 66
Hakanson
 Joseph G, 83-85
Hoff
 Peter, 114, 131
Hutchinson
 Frederick, 100, 105
Jacobson
 George, 113
Katz
 Bennett D, 57, 108, 116-117
King
 Angus S Jr, 46, 65, 85, 101, 109-110, 113, 115-116, 130, 155, 185
 Stephen, 154
Lavigne
 Jean, xiii
Leighton
 Porter D, 83

Every Name Index

Libby
James Delmas, iii, 192
Jennifer Marie, 192
Winthrop, 48
Lick
Dale, 84, 88, 90-91
Lincoln
Abraham, 82
Longley
James B, 46, 54-57, 59-66, 115, 140-146, 156, 173, 175, 182
MacTaggart
Terrence, 46, 65, 85, 106, 112, 114, 116, 118, 120, 122, 129-133, 191
Marsh
Curtis, 117
Martin
John, 87
Masterson
Robert, 61
McCarthy
Patrick E, 46, 56, 66-68, 70-72, 76, 142, 187

McIntire
Prof Walter, xiii
McKernan
John R Jr, 46, 65, 78, 83-85, 89-90, 93-99, 102, 155, 184
McNeil
Donald R, 20, 46-47, 52-56, 59-62, 65-66, 120, 186
Murphy
Thomas W, 74
Muskie
Edmund, 76
Orenduff
J Michael, 46, 85, 93, 102-108, 116, 190
Phillipi
Harlan, 88
Qualia
Russell, 113
Reed
Governor, 48
Reynolds
Thomas Hedley, 80
Rogers
Gil, 84
Sampson
Jean, 58, 144

Scribner
Rodney L, 91
Small
Mary, 106
Smith
Margaret Chase, 66
Strider
Robert, 76
Vamvakias
Sally, 108
Wells
Owen, 71, 72, 130, 146
Weschler
Dean Bart, xiii
Whitman
Christine Todd, 35
Woodbury
Robert L, 46, 74-75, 85-86, 88-93, 96, 100, 109, 118, 189

main
Me.Coll
30.-

378.741 LIBBY   Me.Coll.
Libby, James Delmas
Super U : the history and
politics of the University
of Maine System

	DATE DUE	
JUN 0 7 2002		